THE WELL-PLANNED GARDEN

SUE PHILLIPS

WEIDENFELD & NICOLSON
New York

Published by Weidenfeld & Nicolson, New York
A Division of Wheatland Corporation
10 East 53rd Street
New York, New York 10022

Created and produced by Phoebe Phillips Editions

Designers: Rachael Foster, Phil Kay

Illustrators: Lee Travis (main gardens)
Jennifer Abbott
Emma Sharp
Siân Walters

US consultant: Anne M. Halpin

Library of Congress Cataloging-in-Publication Data

Phillips, Sue.
    The well-planned garden.

    1. Gardens—Design. 2. Landscape gardening.
I. Title.
SB473.P495   1988   635.9   87–34693
ISBN 1–55584–189–9

First Edition

10 9 8 7 6 5 4 3 2 1

CONTENTS

Introduction

The Well-Planned Garden contains 60 plans for a variety of gardens ranging from herbaceous borders to conifer beds, rose gardens to woodland clearings.

Once you have chosen the plan you like, it is simply a matter of following individual instructions: *The Well-Planned Garden* shows that you don't have to be a dedicated gardener to have a beautiful garden, in the same way that you don't have to be a chef to follow a recipe. And, just like a cookbook, it is arranged as a series of recipes – for a variety of gardens.

There are twelve self-contained chapters, each consisting of a garden plus four variations. The main recipe starts with a list of ingredients – the plants you will need, season by season, and also exact quantities of materials like garden fertilizer and compost, that you will require for your first year's gardening, plus a list of necessary tools: everything that's needed to create the garden.

The method that follows takes you through the seasons with detailed, step-by-step instructions on how to plant (from the depth of the hole you dig to the kind of dressing you add to the soil), when and exactly how to prune or deadhead the flowers, which plants need supporting, how to cut back and tidy up individual plants when autumn and winter come. . . . Planting instructions are in the tinted column.

The plants used in this 'main recipe' are shown individually at the opening of each chapter linked to the list of ingredients, and impressionistically combined in an illustration of the bed or border at the start of the method. This, in turn, is linked with a planting plan on which colored areas indicate which plants are in bloom at the height of the flowering season (where relevant – herbs, for example, are not grown primarily for their flowers). This is an ideal: flowering times can vary according to local weather conditions, the micro-climate in your garden – even the plant's situation and when it is planted. For correct distances between plants, follow the positioning of the plant numbers on the plan.

In the variations that follow, some or, occasionally, all the plants are replaced to create different effects. These include new color schemes and shapes, easy care or scented versions, and gardens that are suitable for specific sites – shade or sun.

In the plans that accompany the variations, replacement plants are shown in yellow, with flowering times given in the caption. Maintenance information and quantities (in the variation ingredients) are given for these plants only. Check with the main recipe for instructions on how to tend the remaining (original) plants and how many of them to buy.

Most individual plants are drawn to scale although, in cases where leaf or flower shapes or texture are important, a detail is sometimes shown rather than the entire plant. Each plant falls into one of the following height categories:

Dwarf: up to 12 inches
Short: from 12 inches to 3 feet
Medium: from 3 feet to 6 feet
Tall: over 6 feet

A word about plant names

Latin plant names enable gardeners in all parts of the world to speak a common language, and they are used throughout the book in the lists of ingredients. Names are abbreviated when this is the form in which they are commonly known. Frequently used common names are in brackets in the ingredient lists; these and other, more unusual, ones are given in the index.

Timing operations

Maintenance instructions take you through the gardening year, season by season. Remember, though, that these dates are averages and, like flowering times, can be affected by local weather conditions and even your garden's micro-climate. Check with the zone map on the inside of the back cover and, if you live in an area where temperatures are either extremely high or extremely low, check flowering and planting times with your garden center when you buy plants.

Be guided by what the plant tells you. When it starts to grow (usually, when it is available from garden centers) is the best time to plant it; the time to cut it back is when it starts to die back naturally. Similarly, if the winter has been a hard one, delay pruning in spring for a few weeks until the weather improves.

Many gardeners prefer to do an entire planting job at once, and conventional planting times are therefore not always followed in this book: some of the herbs in Herb Gardens could in fact be planted earlier than late spring; roses are normally planted in late winter to early spring when they are dormant, but we occasionally suggest using container-grown specimens and planting them in spring with other plants in a plan.

Additional reminders for continuing care are in boxes and start 'In subsequent years. . . .' Other extra information, also in boxes, is headed 'Special note'.

Soil preparation

Preparing soil can be anything from a major to a relatively minor undertaking.

If a site has not been cultivated before, you will need to work material in to improve the soil. This is especially necessary if it is sandy or clay soil, because plants do not generally grow well in these conditions. Peat is often used, but can be expensive if there is a large area to treat. If you live in an area where farmyard or stable manure is available, this can be used provided it is very well rotted. You can also make your own soil improver by composting garden rubbish in a heap or a special compost bin until it resembles good soil.

To dig soil properly, do not just turn over the top layer to the depth of the spade – go deeper.

Start by digging out a trench the width of your spade right across the plot. Stack the soil in a heap near the far end of the plot; you'll be needing it later. Use a fork to loosen the soil at the bottom of the trench, then put a layer of peat, manure or compost in the bottom of it. Now take the spade again and dig a second row to form a new trench alongside the first, using the soil from the new trench to fill in the old one.

As you dig, turn the soil over so it lands in the trench upside down, burying any annual weeds in the process. If you spot any thick white roots, pull them out and throw them into a bucket – the chances are they will be perennial weeds which need to be disposed of. Continue working your way backwards across the plot, digging a new trench and filling in the old one each time. When you have dug your way across the plot, use the soil from the first trench to fill in the last one.

As an alternative, you can rent a rototiller to do the digging although, in actual fact, using a rototiller is not much less effort than digging in the first place. Unless you have a large and powerful model, you may find that it does not dig deeply but just skims the surface. If you doubt your capabilities, hire an experienced operator to come and do the tilling for you. He'll know the technique for getting the best out of it.

Ground that has been deeply dug before, and regularly cultivated since, does not need so much effort. Simply spread peat, manure or compost in a layer over the surface – the rate varies slightly according to what you are going to plant, but on average allow 2 × 2 gallon bucketfuls per square yard. Work backwards across the plot as before and dig so that as the soil from each row is turned over, the compost on top of it is turned under and buried.

When you have finished digging the soil should be roughly level, but it will be covered in large clods. These must be broken up before plants can be put in. To do this, use a rake in long sweeping movements backwards and forwards. The teeth break the lumps into a fine, level tilth, and collect up stones as they go. Stop periodically and gather the largest stones into a bucket, to get rid of them later.

Fertilizer should ideally be spread a few days before you intend to plant the plot. For most gardens in this book, I suggest you spread 5–10–5 fertilizer at a rate of 2 to 3 pounds per 100 square feet and rake it in, leaving the soil level. Sprinkle the products at the manufacturer's recommended rate and make sure to get them as evenly spread as possible. If you find it difficult to distribute granules evenly, you'll find it helps to mark the plot out into squares of approximately 1 yard and deal with each one individually. After treating the whole area, rake the soil lightly so the granules are mixed into the surface.

On clay soils, incorporate ground limestone at the rate of 5 pounds per 100 square feet, as well as a 3 inch layer of peat, compost or manure, if you are working with herbaceous plants: their roots remain in the ground over winter and can easily rot in heavy clay soil.

When growing plants that are specifically acid or alkali loving, it is a good idea to check the pH factor of your soil. Small soil test kits are inexpensive and easily available from garden centers. To collect a good soil sample, take a trowel and plastic bag and dig a series of holes to the full depth of the trowel, all over the area to be planted. Scoop a small sample of soil from the bottom of each hole and mix all the samples together in the plastic bag. Remove a small quantity to test.

The pH scale runs from 0 to 14 and measures how acid or alkaline the soil is (0 is the most acid, 7 is neutral and 14 the most alkaline). Most plants grow best when the pH is around 6.0 to 6.5.

After planting

When you have finished planting it is advisable to spread a thin layer of peat or well-rotted garden compost or manure between the plants. Mulching, as this is called, has many beneficial effects; it smothers weed seedlings, improves the soil by adding organic matter to it, insulates the roots of the plants from heat in summer and cold in winter and helps to retain moisture in the soil (particularly important in the case of annuals, which are very shallow-rooted). It also provides a pleasingly uniform dark background for the plants. Mulch again every spring as the growing season begins.

Watering

When your garden is newly planted, you must make sure that your plants receive sufficient water. This is particularly important in the case of bedding plants which, being shallow-rooted, are very vulnerable to the top layer of soil drying out. After about a month, when the roots have penetrated deeper into the soil, looking at its surface is no longer enough. You need to either stick your finger or the probe of an electronic meter into the soil to a depth of 3–4 inches. If you are still unsure, dig out a handful of soil to the depth of the trowel and inspect it for moisture.

Weeding

Perennial garden weeds like couch grass, nettles, thistles and docks can be eradicated either by hand or with chemicals. Hand-weeding is slower because after the weeds are dug or pulled, fragments of root often remain and the weeds grow back. This is particularly true with couch grass, where digging up is akin to a form of propagation. However, hand-weeding is still the safest way to get rid of weeds.

Chemical herbicides come in powder, spray, or stick form, and are available in varying strengths. Stick weedkillers are best for spot applications. Powders are usually spread and then worked in. Read the label of whatever product you use to check on handling instructions and safe planting times.

Pests and diseases

These are the bane of every gardener's life and the first rule is: know your enemy. Accordingly, here is a list of the most common problems you can expect to affect the planting schemes in this book.

Aphids Also known as greenfly, blackfly and plant lice, these pests feed on plant sap, thus distorting young growth. They also leave behind them a sticky dew which attracts black mold. They are round-bodied insects which may be green, brown, cream or pink and they are particularly fond of roses, where they can be found clustering on the growing stems and buds. Spray them with nicotine, malathion, pyrethrum or insecticidal soap.

Blackspot This is a rose disease which generally appears in late spring, manifesting itself as black spots on the leaves. Remove and burn the affected leaves and spray every two weeks with a rose fungicide. Apply a foliar feed, as the disease is worse on weak, unhealthy plants.

Mildew This looks like a dusting of talcum powder which appears in small patches and then spreads, distorting the plant. It is particularly prevalent in cool, humid weather – keep a watch for it in poor summers and in early autumn. Spray with Benlate or copper fungicide.

Pesticides

There are two different kinds of pesticide – contact and systemic. Contact sprays are applied direct to the insects, whereas systemic insecticides are absorbed into the plant, subsequently killing the insects which feed upon it. Systemic insecticides cannot be washed off by rain.

Chemical sprays are highly toxic, so always follow the manufacturer's instructions to the letter. Never mix them unless instructed to do so; dispose of any surplus and wash out the sprayer thoroughly.

As a first line of defense, spray with insecticidal soap before using chemicals.

Pruning

This is a subject that can cause much anguish among novice gardeners. Instructions are given for the individual plants in this book but as a general rule the main purpose of pruning is to maintain a good shape and to remove any weak or dead shoots. To check whether a shoot is dead or not, look at the inside of it. If it is dead it will be a dull brown color, while a live, healthy shoot will be a green or creamy color inside. When you are removing dead shoots, cut back cleanly to just above a live bud so that there is no dead wood left to encourage further die-back.

Special notes

● Unless otherwise stated in the instructions, always use pruning shears for pruning and trimming.

● Replacement and additional plants are given at the start of each variation. For quantities of original plants, check with the list at the start of the main plan.

Mixed Borders

They don't look contrived, but the best mixed borders are carefully planned. Here an average-sized bed has been landscaped. Although roses are normally planted in early spring, it makes sense, in this case, to buy container-grown plants and put them in at the same time as the others in the border.

This planting scheme needs a reasonably sunny but slightly sheltered site. The bed should have a wall or fence along the back, but you could put up posts and wires, trellis or plastic-coated wire.

Ingredients for a border 15 foot × 4 foot

Mid spring

12 *Lathyrus odoratus* 'Jet Set Mixed' (sweet peas)

5 *Digitalis purpurea* (foxglove)

2 *Astilbe × arendsii* 'Fanal'

3 *Delphinium* 'Pacific Hybrids'

1 Floribunda rose 'Pinocchio'

5 *Lilium regale* (lily)

3 *Aquilegia* 'McKana Hybrids' (columbine)

2 *Hosta sieboldiana* 'Elegans'

1 *Artemisia abrotanum*

1 Climbing rose 'Golden Showers'

2 *Armeria maritima*

8 *Antirrhinum* 'Floral Carpet' (snapdragon)

3 *Dianthus* 'Doris'

Late spring

12 *Lobelia erinus* 'Mrs. Clibran'

9 *Nicotiana alata* 'Sensation Mixed'

5 *Petunia multiflora* 'Resisto Mixed'

5 *Tagetes patula* (marigold)

From the garden shed

Slug traps and bait, if necessary

12 × 8 foot high brushwood sticks

3 × 7 foot high plant stakes

Plant ties

20 × 2 gallon bucketfuls of peat, garden compost or well-rotted manure

Tools required

Spade

Garden fork

Rake

Garden line

Hand trowel

Watering can or hose

Pruning shears

Lawn shears

Hoe (optional)

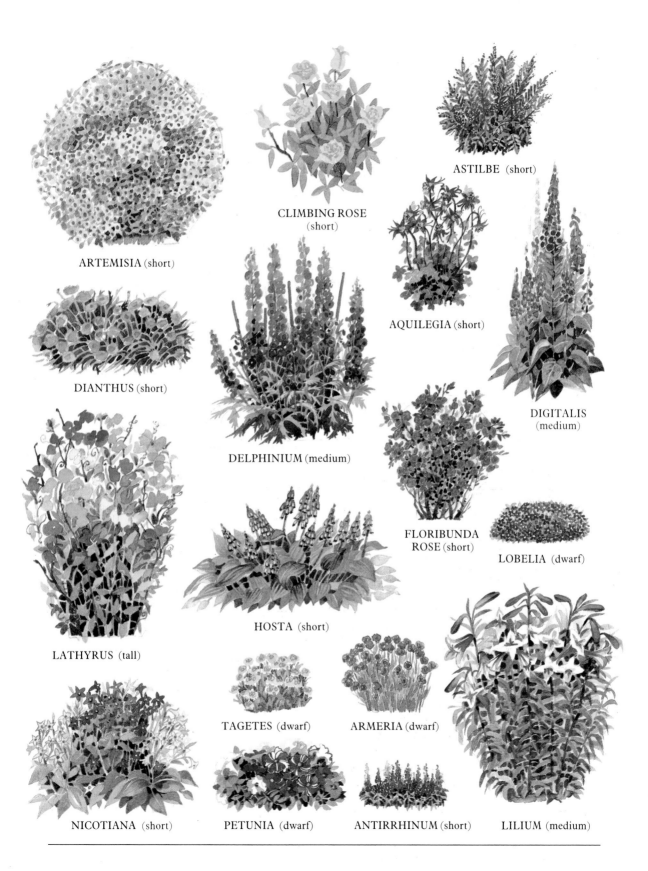

ARTEMISIA (short)

CLIMBING ROSE
(short)

ASTILBE (short)

AQUILEGIA (short)

DIANTHUS (short)

DELPHINIUM (medium)

DIGITALIS
(medium)

FLORIBUNDA
ROSE (short)

LOBELIA (dwarf)

LATHYRUS (tall)

HOSTA (short)

TAGETES (dwarf)

ARMERIA (dwarf)

NICOTIANA (short)

PETUNIA (dwarf)

ANTIRRHINUM (short)

LILIUM (medium)

Method

Before buying your plants, prepare the ground and have everything ready. Start by marking out the bed with the garden line. Cut alongside the line with the spade to form the boundary of the border. Use the spade the wrong way around so the blade goes into the soil at right angles – this gives you a nice clean edge to the grass in front of the bed which can easily be kept tidy with lawn shears later. Remove the line and prepare the soil, applying the peat, manure or compost at the rate of 2 bucketfuls per square yard of bed (see introduction).

Mid spring

Before planting   Water the roses, sweet peas, foxgloves, astilbe, delphiniums, columbines, hosta, artemisia, armeria, snapdragons and dianthus 12 hours before you intend to plant them.

Prune the roses. Use sharp pruning shears to cut back the stems of the floribunda rose, Pinocchio, to approximately 6 inches above the top of the pot. Cut the strongest stems of the climber down to 12 inches above the top of the pot, and cut the weaker stems to 4 inches. Always cut just above the place where a leaf joins the stem.

Planting   Set the roses, foxgloves, astilbe, delphiniums, columbines, hosta, artemisia, armeria and dianthus out on the bed, still in their pots, in their planting positions. Turn them so that their best side faces the front of the bed.

Plant from the back of the bed towards the front. This way you are less likely to tread on any plants and, most importantly, it gives you the chance to scuff over footprints with the trowel.

Lift each pot in turn and mark its exact position with the trowel. Dig a small hole the same depth as the pot in the position you have marked, then knock the plants out of their pots. They will come out quite easily if you tap the base of the pots with the trowel first. If they are growing in flexible plastic containers, these should be cut away carefully without disturbing the ball of roots inside.

MAINTENANCE

If slugs are a problem in your garden, set out baited slug traps and check them regularly.

Water whenever necessary, starting the day after planting. Check to see if it is needed by looking at the surface of the soil. If it has dried out, then water again. Do this regularly every few days in dry weather and about once a week if there is some natural rainfall.

Continue watering like this for the first two or three weeks until you can see the plants growing. This indicates that they are becoming established.

In subsequent years, in **early spring**, prune the roses. Use sharp pruning shears and cut any dead or very thin, weak shoots out entirely, back to the base. Then cut all the stems of the floribunda rose, Pinocchio, down to 8 inches. To prune the climbing rose, cut back the short shoots that carried last year's flowers to within a few inches of the main stem they are growing from. Always cut just above a leaf joint.

As the climbing rose grows bigger, train in new branches to extend the basic framework until the space allocated for the plant is finally filled, with branches spaced evenly over the area. From then on, you will be able to select the best of the new branches to replace some of the older ones. The latter are recognizable by their dark-colored bark, whereas young shoots have lighter brown or greenish skin. Simply cut out the old branch completely to a convenient junction with another stem and tie the new branch in its place.

Above Mixed border. **Below** Plan for the border. Colored areas indicate flowers in bloom in mid summer. Average flowering periods are listed below:

1 *Sweet peas*: Early spring–early autumn **2** *Lobelia*: Early summer–early autumn
3 *Nicotiana*: Mid summer–late summer **4** *Foxgloves*: Early summer–mid summer
5 *Astilbe*: Early summer–mid summer **6** *Petunias*: Early summer–late summer
7 *Delphiniums*: Early summer–mid summer **8** *Floribunda rose*: Early summer–mid summer **9** *Tagetes*: Early summer–early autumn **10** *Hostas*: Mid summer–late summer
11 *Lilies*: Early summer **12** *Artemisia*: Early summer–mid summer **13** *Climbing rose*: Early summer–late summer **14** *Snapdragons*: Early summer–late summer **15** *Armeria*: Late spring–mid summer **16** *Dianthus*: Early summer **17** *Columbine*: Mid spring–late spring

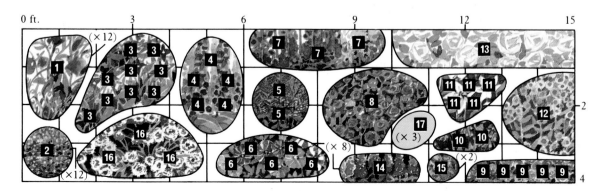

(Mid spring)

Taking great care not to break up the rootball, place the plant into its hole. Check that the top of the rootball is level with the surrounding soil, as it is important not to put it any deeper than the plant was growing in its pot. If it is not level, add or remove some soil from the bottom of the hole until it is right.

Make sure the best side of the plant is still facing the front, and give it a slight turn if not. Fill in around the roots with soil. Very lightly firm around the plant with the trowel handle.

The sweet peas and snapdragons will be supplied growing in trays or 'strips'. Thin or flimsy trays can be torn away, but rigid ones are best removed by giving the base a couple of sharp taps on a concrete path, and then tipping the contents gently out. You will find the roots have grown together into a tangled mass. Separate the individual plants by tearing the soil apart so that each of the plants is left with an approximately equal-sized rootball. Lay these plants in their planting positions.

To plant them, lift each one and mark its position with the trowel as before. Dig a hole wide enough to take the ball of roots, but about 1 inch deeper. Plant as before, but this time ensure that the rootball is buried slightly below the soil surface – about 1 inch, no more. This is to give the plant a little support and help it to stay upright.

To plant the lily bulbs, dig a hole 9 inches deep for each bulb. Set the bulb at the bottom of the hole, with the pointed end up, and press it gently into the soil. Fill in the hole.

Water the plants in. This is to settle the soil round the roots, as well as to help them start growing. Give each of the roses $\frac{1}{2}$ gallon of water, other plants 1 pint of water each.

In subsequent years, fork over the ground each spring, using the points of the fork to loosen the soil lightly rather than actually turn it over as this would disturb shallow-rooted plants.

Apply fertilizer evenly over the surface of the bed. You can use 5–10–5 at a rate of 2–3 pounds per 100 square feet, or alternatively buy any good fertilizer and follow the instructions on the package. Hoe the fertilizer in after scattering it and give the bed a thorough soaking with the hose if the soil is dry.

Divide hosta and astilbe when the clumps become large and overcrowded. The easiest way to do this is to dig them out of the ground, stick two garden forks into the middle of the clump, back to back, and lever them apart. If the pieces are still rather large, repeat the operation. Replant the pieces with lots of young shoots from the outside of the original clump.

Mulch the entire bed each year for weed control and to minimize watering. If, however, you prefer to use another method of weed control you should still mulch around the hosta, astilbe and lilies as they need extra moisture around their roots to grow well. Spread a thin layer of garden compost or well-rotted manure in a 12 inch circle around each plant. Water well before mulching if the ground is at all dry, and take care not to break off any of the young shoots.

If slugs are a problem in your garden, set out baited slug traps around new plants and hostas to protect them from damage.

Special note

When you have finished planting it is advisable to spread a thin layer of garden compost or well-rotted manure between the plants. Mulching, as this is called, has many beneficial effects; it smothers weed seedlings, improves the soil by adding organic matter to it, insulates the roots of the plants from heat in summer and cold in winter and helps to retain moisture in the soil (particularly important in the case of annuals, which are very shallow-rooted). It also provides a pleasingly uniform dark background to the plants. Mulch again every spring as the growing season begins.

Late spring

Plant the nicotiana, lobelia, petunia and marigolds after all danger of frost has passed, following the same method as for sweet peas and snapdragons.

Support sweet pea plants by pushing brushwood sticks in among them.

They may need a little encouragement to start climbing, but once they do they will manage without further help as their tendrils cling to the sticks.

Check slug traps regularly if you use them. Empty the contents and add new bait as necessary.

Continue to water frequently in dry weather.

Early summer

Deadhead regularly. Go over the bed once a week snipping off the dead flowers as close to the head as possible with sharp scissors or pruning shears.

Cut columbine flower stems down to ground level, after they have flowered.

When deadheading roses, cut the old flower heads off a short way down the stem, just above a healthy, full-sized leaf. A new shoot will then grow from a tiny bud in the angle where the leaf joins the stem, and it is from this that the next flush of flowers will come.

Weed the bed every two weeks to keep it tidy. If you prefer to use a hoe, be very careful – all the plants in the bed except the roses have very soft stems and are easily cut into or broken off by careless hoeing.

Keep weeds down by mulching; spread a thin layer of garden compost or well-rotted manure all over the surface of the bed between the plants. This will smother weed seedlings as soon as they germinate, but you do have to start with weed-free ground, so hoe before mulching. It will also help the soil to retain moisture, provided you water the soil thoroughly beforehand.

Trim the grass round the edge of the bed if it is set in

(Early summer)

a lawn. Each time you mow the grass, cut neatly round the edge of the border with lawn shears to give a clean finish.

Spray the roses with insecticide against aphids (greenfly) whenever necessary. Examine the plants every week or two to see if they have become infested with these insects, which are very common. They will usually be found in groups living on young shoots, flower buds and the undersides of young leaves towards the top of the plant. Despite their common name, greenfly may also be brown, cream or even pink.

It is also advisable to spray roses regularly against blackspot, another common problem. This is a fungal disease which produces characteristic black spotty marks on the foliage. If you want to keep your plants free of this you will need to spray them with a special rose fungicide every two weeks (or as directed in the manufacturer's instructions).

Train the climbing rose over the wall or fence at the back of the border or, alternatively, over the netting, wires or trellis you have put up especially for it. The idea is to encourage its stems to grow out and form a framework that roughly covers the area you want it to fill. Once this basic framework of branches has been established it is very easy to keep the plant properly organized. Tie the branches in place with plant ties to form what will eventually become this permanent framework.

Mid summer

Deadhead the delphiniums when the flowers finish blooming. Cut the dead flowers off partway down the stem, just above a healthy-looking leaf. In this way you can sometimes coax the plants to produce a few more flowers. After you finish, remove the dead flower heads from the bed. Cut out the central flowering spike of digitalis, after flowering, to encourage flowering side shoots to increase in size.

You may wish to remove the flowers of artemisia, as the shrub is grown for its grey felty leaves which set off the flowers around it.

Continue with the jobs described above: watering, providing protection against slugs, weeding, trimming the edge of the border, and spraying and training the roses.

Late summer	Continue watering if necessary, checking slug traps if you use them, weeding, trimming, and spraying and training the roses.
Early autumn	Deadhead the floribunda rose, which in a good summer will be producing a second flush of flowers now. Spray the roses against mildew. This disease is easy to recognize – it looks as if someone has dusted talcum powder over the leaves, stems and flower buds. As it gets worse large areas of the plant may be covered and some of the leaves may even be shed. Mildew can often be a problem in autumn when the weather is dull, cool and humid. Spray with the rose fungicide you used in summer to prevent blackspot. Repeat every two weeks. Towards the end of September, cut down and remove the dead flower stems and foliage from the lilies when they start to die back naturally. Cut down the flower stems and leaves of the delphiniums, hostas, columbines and astilbes to ground level after they have finished flowering and the leaves start to turn yellow. Pull out sweet peas, marigolds, petunia, nicotiana and lobelia after all their flowers are finished. Clear any weeds, plant stakes and other debris from the bed.

> **In subsequent years**, prune artemisia by cutting out any damaged or straggly shoots. Cut the flower stems back to just above a convenient leaf if you allowed the plant to flower. Armeria and dianthus may need light pruning: select straggly or broken shoots and cut right back to base.

Mid autumn	Give the floribunda rose a light pruning. All that is necessary is to shorten the stems by about half. This removes most of the leafy growth that would otherwise get blown about by the wind or broken by snow during the winter. Remove the prunings, give the bed a final weeding and leave it tidy ready for winter. Spray the roses against mildew every two weeks. If you live where winters are cold, prepare the base with an 8–10 inch mound of soil, covered with 8–10 inches of loose mulch. Cut digitalis to ground level and pull out snapdragons after the flowers are over.

Low Maintenance

A traditional mixed border, like the one in the main plan, calls for a certain amount of work. You can, however, have a mixed border without needing to prune roses, train climbers and replace annuals every year, simply by changing these plants for low-maintenance substitutes. This variation is a mixed border that creates a similar visual effect, but needs very much less work.

Mid spring

2 *Sedum* × 'Autumn Joy' (replace *Lathyrus odoratus* 'Jet Set Mixed')

1 *Ruta graveolens* (replaces *Lobelia erinus* 'Mrs. Clibran')

4 *Lupinus* 'Russell Hybrids' (replace *Nicotiana alata* 'Sensation Mixed')

3 *Nepeta* × *faassenii* (replace *Tagetes patula*)

3 *Ajuga reptans* (replace *Petunia multiflora* 'Resisto Mixed')

1 Shrub rose 'Bonica' (replaces 'Pinocchio')

1 *Lonicera japonica* 'Halliana' (honeysuckle) (replaces 'Golden Showers')

3 *Alchemilla mollis* (replace *Armeria maritima* and *Antirrhinum* 'Floral Carpet')

From the garden shed

8 × 2½ foot high stakes, if you live in a windy area

SHRUB ROSE (short)

LUPINUS (short)

LONICERA (medium)

RUTA (short)

NEPETA (short)

AJUGA (dwarf)

ALCHEMILLA (short)

SEDUM (short)

Mid spring Prepare the bed and plant, following the method described on page 10. The rose needs no pruning before planting except to cut out any dead or very weak shoots.

> **In subsequent years**, snap off the old flower stems of sedum when growth begins. Trim ruta back to old (dark) wood to preserve its bushy shape.

Late spring Push stakes in either side of each lupine plant for support if you live in a windy area.

Encourage the honeysuckle to start climbing up on to its supports. Secure the stems in place initially with a few plant ties. Once it has started to climb it will need no further help, as it twines round its supports to hold itself in place.

Early summer Deadhead the shrub rose regularly, as this will encourage it to continue blooming and produce a second flush of flower later in the year. Do not bother removing the flowering stems of artemisia, as the flowers form part of this planting scheme.

Mid summer Remove the dead heads from ajuga after flowering by clipping lightly with shears.

Deadhead lupines when the flowers are faded. Cut the dead flowers off partway down the stem, just above a healthy-looking leaf. You may sometimes coax the plants to produce a few more flowers.

Early autumn Cut down and remove the dead stems and the foliage of nepeta and lupines after flowering, and the stems and old foliage of alchemilla. Leave the new foliage in the centre of the plants. Remove dead flowers from ruta.

> **In subsequent years**, in **mid autumn**, prune honeysuckle only if the plant becomes too big. Simply remove any shoots that are straggly or starting to grow where they are not wanted. Cut just above the place where a leaf joins a stem. Leave dead sedum stems on plants.
>
> The rose does not require regular pruning, but cut out any dead, damaged or overcrowded shoots.

1 *Sedum*: Late summer–mid autumn **2** *Ruta*: Early–mid summer **3** *Lupines*: Late spring–mid summer **4** *Nepeta*: Late spring–early autumn **5** *Ajuga*: Early–mid summer **6** *Shrub rose*: Early–mid summer **7** *Honeysuckle*: Mid summer–mid autumn **8** *Alchemilla*: Early–late summer **9** *Astilbe* **10** *Foxgloves* **11** *Delphiniums* **12** *Lilies* **13** *Hostas* **14** *Artemisia* **15** *Dianthus* **16** *Columbine*

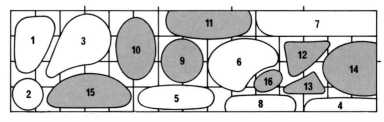

Shady

Most garden plants prefer reasonably sunny locations, but if you have a shady area, opt for this variation which uses shade-loving plants. You will not need any stakes.

Mid spring

3 *Helleborus orientalis* (replace *Lathyrus odoratus* 'Jet Set Mixed')

1 *Euonymus fortunei* 'Emerald 'n' Gold' (replaces *Lobelia erinus* 'Mrs. Clibran')

3 *Aruncus dioicus* (replace *Nicotiana alata* 'Sensation Mixed')

3 *Hosta fortunei* 'Albopicta' (replace *Petunia multiflora* 'Resisto Mixed')

3 *Ligularia stenocephala* 'The Rocket' (replace *Delphinium* 'Pacific Hybrids')

1 *Sambucus canadensis* (replaces 'Pinocchio')

3 *Polygonatum multiflorum* (replace *Lilium regale*)

1 *Mahonia aquifolium* (replaces *Artemisia abrotanum*)

1 *Lonicera japonica* 'Halliana' (honeysuckle) (replaces 'Golden Showers')

3 *Ajuga reptans* (replace *Armeria maritima* and *Antirrhinum* 'Floral Carpet')

3 *Alchemilla mollis* (replace *Tagetes patula*)

4 *Bergenia cordifolia* (replace *Dianthus* 'Doris')

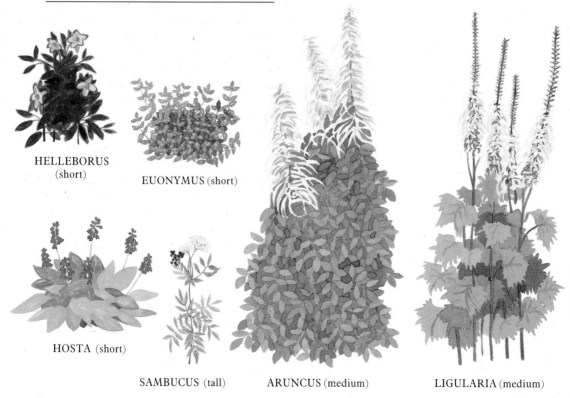

HELLEBORUS (short)

EUONYMUS (short)

HOSTA (short)

SAMBUCUS (tall)

ARUNCUS (medium)

LIGULARIA (medium)

Mid spring   Prepare and plant the bed as previously described on page 10.

POLYGONATUM
(short)

MAHONIA (medium)

ALCHEMILLA
(short)

LONICERA
(medium)

BERGENIA (short)

AJUGA (dwarf)

1 *Helleborus*: Early–late spring
2 *Euonymus*: Late spring–early summer   **3** *Aruncus*: Early summer
4 *Hosta fortunei*: Mid summer
5 *Ligularia*: Mid–late summer
6 *Sambucus*   **7** *Polygonatum*:
Early summer   **8** *Mahonia*:
Early–mid spring   **9** *Honeysuckle*:
Mid summer–mid autumn
10 *Ajuga*: Early–mid summer
11 *Alchemilla*: Early–late summer
12 *Bergenia*: Mid–late spring
13 *Foxgloves*   **14** *Hosta*
15 *Astilbe*   **16** *Columbine*

Early summer   Deadhead bergenia and helleborus by removing the dead flower spikes when all the flowers are finished. Cut the stems down almost to ground level. Do not remove dead flowerheads from mahonia.

Mid summer   Deadhead aruncus, as above, and cut the stems down.

Late summer   Clip the dead heads off ajuga with shears.

Early autumn   Cut the dead flower stems and the old leaves from alchemilla, but leave the new foliage growing in the center of the plants intact. Remove the dead flower spikes from ligularia, and cut the stems down almost to ground level.

In subsequent years, in **early spring**, dig up and divide polygonatum when clumps become too large, as described below (mid spring).

In **mid spring**, dig up and divide bergenia, ligularia, alchemilla, hosta and ajuga plants when the clumps get too big. Use two garden forks back to back to pry the clump apart, and replant only the best pieces with lots of young growth from around the outside of the original clump. Do not, however, treat helleborus this way as the plants dislike being disturbed. When mahonia plants get big, cut a few of the oldest branches to ground level.

In **early autumn**, euonymus may require light pruning – cut entire shoots back to a main branch.

Do not cut bergenia down as it is evergreen, but do remove any leaves that are yellow or dried out.

In **mid autumn**, prune honeysuckle when the plant gets too big by cutting short any straggly or over-long shoots. Cut to just above a leaf joint.

Sambucus is unlikely to require any pruning as this variety is very slow growing, but cut off any dead or broken shoots as soon as they are seen.

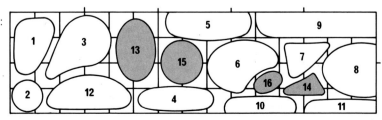

For Flower Arrangers

If you like using flowers indoors, this variation will keep you supplied with something to cut for most of the summer and still leave the garden looking well stocked! Buy the following plants to replace the ones in brackets.

Mid spring

1 *Anaphalis triplinervis* (replaces *Lobelia erinus* 'Mrs. Clibran')

5 *Achillea taygetea* 'Moonshine' (replace *Digitalis purpurea*)

3 *Hosta fortunei* 'Albopicta' (replace *Petunia multiflora* 'Resisto Mixed')

1 *Gypsophila paniculata* 'Bristol Fairy' (replaces *Artemisia abronatum*)

3 *Alchemilla mollis* (replace *Armeria maritima* and *Antirrhinum* 'Floral Carpet')

2 *Astrantia maxima* (replace *Tagetes patula*)

Late spring

9 *Nicotiana alata* 'Lime Green' (replace *Nicotiana alata* 'Sensation Mixed')

From the garden shed

12 stakes

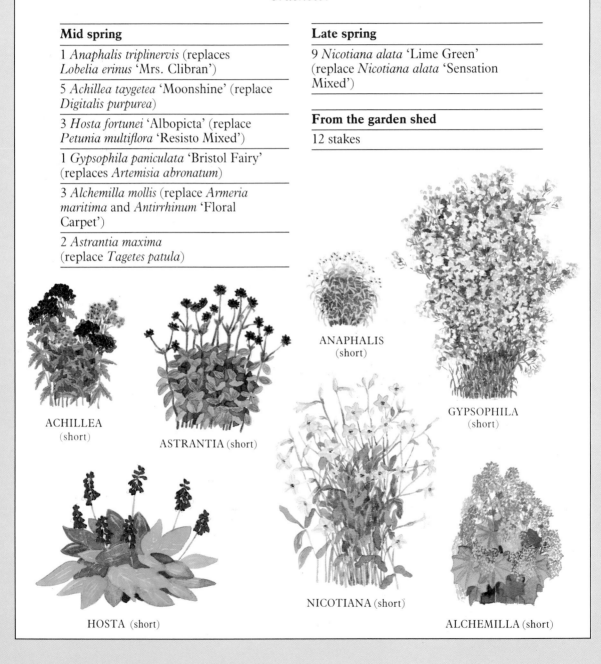

ACHILLEA
(short)

ASTRANTIA (short)

ANAPHALIS
(short)

GYPSOPHILA
(short)

HOSTA (short)

NICOTIANA (short)

ALCHEMILLA (short)

Mid spring   Prepare the bed and plant the anaphalis, achillea, hosta, gypsophila, alchemilla and astrantia as described on page 10.

Late spring   Plant the nicotiana following the method described on page 12 after the date of the last expected frost in your area.

> **In subsequent years**, replant nicotiana annually.

Push a few stakes in around the gypsophila to support the plant if you live in a windy area.

Push a few stakes in around the nicotiana for support if you live in a windy area.

> **In subsequent years**, dig up and divide hostas, following the instructions for bergenia etc on page 19.

Early to mid summer   Cut astrantia flowers for drying soon after they open. Hang the flowers upside down in small bunches in a cool airy place out of direct sunlight.

Cut flowers that will be used fresh shortly after the buds open. Only cut a few at a time from each plant to avoid spoiling the appearance of the garden in the first year. When the plants are established, you can cut more.

Late summer   Cut anaphalis flowers for drying soon after they open, and dry as described above.

Early autumn   Towards the end of September, cut down the flower stems and foliage of anaphalis, achillea, gypsophila, astrantia and hosta, and remove only the stems and old leaves of alchemilla.

Pull out nicotiana when the last flowers are over.

Remove stakes if these were used as plant supports and leave the bed tidy for winter.

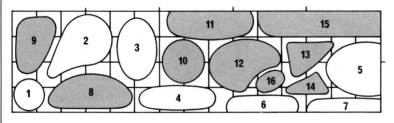

1 *Anaphalis*: Late summer   **2** *Nicotiana*: Mid summer–late summer   **3** *Achillea*: Mid summer–late summer   **4** *Hosta fortunei*: Mid summer   **5** *Gypsophila*: Early summer–late summer   **6** *Alchemilla*: Early summer–late summer   **7** *Astrantia*   **8** *Dianthus*   **9** *Sweet peas*   **10** *Astilbe*   **11** *Delphiniums*   **12** *Floribunda*   **13** *Lilies*   **14** *Hosta sieboldiana*   **15** *Climbing rose*   **16** *Columbine*

Nutrient-Poor

The final variation shows how to turn problem soil into an asset by creating an inspiring and colorful border with plants that will thrive on dry, lifeless soil. Choose a sunny but slightly sheltered site. You will not need any stakes or plant ties for this variation.

Mid spring

4 *Hedera helix* 'Baltica' (replace *Lathyrus odoratus* 'Jet Set Mixed')

4 *Lavandula spica* 'Hidcote' (lavender) (replace *Nicotiana alata* 'Sensation Mixed')

1 *Rosmarinus officinalis* (rosemary) (replaces *Digitalis purpurea*)

1 *Coreopsis lanceolata* 'New Gold' (replaces *Astilbe × arendsii* 'Fanal')

3 *Stachys lanata* (replace *Petunia multiflora* 'Resisto Mixed')

4 *Bergenia cordifolia* (replace *Delphinium* 'Pacific Hybrids')

1 *Sambucus canadensis* (replaces 'Pinocchio')

3 *Liatris spicata* 'Kobold' (replace *Lilium regale*)

1 *Salvia superba* 'East Friesland' (replaces *Hosta sieboldiana* 'Elegans')

4 *Hedera helix* 'Baltica' (replace 'Golden Showers')

3 *Armeria maritima* (replace *Antirrhinum* 'Floral Carpet')

Early summer

5 *Mesembryanthemum* 'Magic Carpet Mixed' (replace *Tagetes patula*)

5 *Portulaca grandiflora* (replace *Lobelia erinus* 'Mrs. Clibran')

From the garden shed

1 × 2 gallon bucketful well-rotted garden compost for mulching

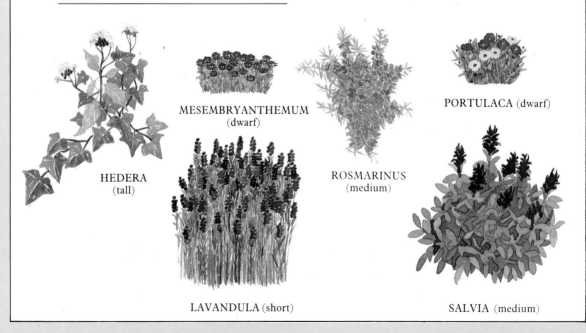

HEDERA
(tall)

MESEMBRYANTHEMUM
(dwarf)

ROSMARINUS
(medium)

PORTULACA (dwarf)

LAVANDULA (short)

SALVIA (medium)

Mid spring   Prepare the border and plant the hedera, lavender, rosemary, coreopsis, stachys, bergenia, sambucus, salvia and armeria following the instructions for astilbe etc on page 10.

Plant the liatris tubers at 2½ times their own depth. After planting and watering in, mulch over the tubers with a bucket of compost to retain moisture round the roots as they grow, then mark the spot with a few short sticks so you do not accidentally hoe them out.

In subsequent years, dig up and divide liatris and bergenia when the clumps become too big. Use two garden forks back to back to pry the clump apart and replant only the best, healthiest-looking pieces with lots of young growth from around the outside of the original clump.

Prune rosemary only to remove any shoots that have been damaged by cold during the winter (these will have turned brown) and to trim any branches that are growing out of shape. In both cases cut the shoots back to their base. No other pruning is necessary.

Remove any shoots of hedera that have broken, come down off their support or turned brown. Cut them off just above a healthy leaf.

Sambucus and salvia need no regular pruning; just cut any damaged or dead shoots back to the junction with a healthy shoot.

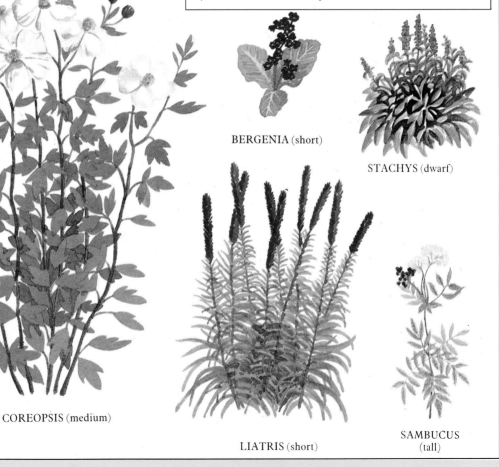

COREOPSIS (medium)

BERGENIA (short)

STACHYS (dwarf)

LIATRIS (short)

SAMBUCUS (tall)

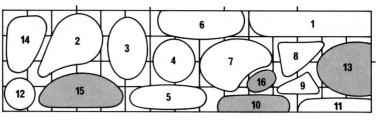

1 *Hedera*   **2** *Lavender*: Early summer–late summer
3 *Rosemary*: Early spring–mid spring   **4** *Coreopsis*: Mid summer–early autumn
5 *Stachys*: Mid summer
6 *Bergenia*: Mid spring–late spring
7 *Sambucus*   **8** *Liatris*: Mid summer–early autumn   **9** *Salvia*
10 *Armeria*: Late spring–mid summer   **11** *Mesembryanthemum*: Early summer–early autumn
12 *Portulaca*: Early summer–late summer   **13** *Artemisia*   **14** *Sedum*
15 *Dianthus*   **16** *Columbine*

Early summer   Plant out the mesembryanthemum and portulaca following the instructions for sweet peas on page 12.

In subsequent years, replace portulaca and mesembryanthemum each year.

Late spring   Train hedera up on to the wall, fence or trellis provided for it. Once it has started to climb the plant is entirely self supporting by means of the aerial roots produced from its climbing stems.

Deadhead bergenia regularly to encourage further flowers.

Spray hedera growing on a wall with plain water from a hose to help the aerial roots to grip into the brickwork. An occasional spraying will be beneficial to hedera growing on fencing, trellis or netting as well, as it will freshen it up.

Deadhead mesembryanthemum and portulaca to encourage further flowers to develop.

Mid summer   Deadhead stachys, liatris, mesembryanthemum and portulaca.

Late summer   Deadhead armeria after all the flowers are over by clipping them off with shears, and continue deadheading the liatris, mesembryanthemum and portulaca.

Early autumn   Cut down the flower stems of liatris and stachys close to the ground when the flowers are over.

Clip lavender with shears to remove the dead flower heads and lightly reshape the plants. Do not cut back into the old wood (easily recognizable by its dark color) or the plants may be killed.

Pull out mesembryanthemum and portulaca when the last of the flowers are over.

Mid autumn   Towards the end of October, cut down the stems of coreopsis almost to ground level and cover the roots with two bucketfuls of peat moss or compost to protect them from frost during the winter.

Perennial Flower Beds

For a garden that is a mass of flowers year after year without needing yearly replanting you can't beat perennial flowers. This plan shows how to create an eyecatching perennial bed that will always be packed with blooms throughout spring, summer and autumn.
Strictly speaking, herbaceous perennials are those that die down in the winter and grow up again each spring. However, the term has become extended slightly to include many sorts of low shrubby plants like helianthemum that in normal cultivation are cut back hard every autumn.

Ingredients for an island bed 12 foot × 13 foot

Mid spring

2 *Acanthus mollis*

3 *Delphinium* 'Pacific Hybrids'

3 *Rudbeckia fulgida* 'Goldsturm'

2 *Phlox paniculata* 'Marlborough'

3 *Coreopsis verticillata*

3 *Hosta fortunei* 'Albopicta'

3 *Lupinus* 'Russell Hybrids'

1 *Gypsophila paniculata* 'Bristol Fairy'

3 *Geum chiloense* 'Mrs. Bradshaw'

3 *Helianthemum nummularium*

3 *Sedum spectabile* 'Autumn Joy'

3 *Alchemilla mollis*

2 *Solidago canadensis* 'Golden Sun'

3 *Campanula carpatica* 'Jingle Bells'

2 *Nepeta* × *faassenii*

5 *Polygonum affine*

From the garden shed

Slug traps and bait, if necessary

12 × 2 gallon bucketfuls of garden compost, leaf mold or bark chips for mulching

3 × 7 foot plant stakes

Bundle of 2½ foot long twigs or slender stakes

Tools required

Spade

Garden fork

Rake

Garden line

Hand trowel

Hose or lawn sprinkler

Hoe

String or plant ties

Pruning shears

Shears

ALCHEMILLA (short)

DELPHINIUM (medium)

HOSTA (short)

COREOPSIS (short)

SEDUM (short)

PHLOX
(short)

CAMPANULA (dwarf)

RUDBECKIA (short)

LUPINUS (short)

NEPETA (short)

POLYGONUM (dwarf)

GEUM (short)

ACANTHUS
(short)

GYPSOPHILA
(short)

HELIANTHEMUM (dwarf)

SOLIDAGO
(medium)

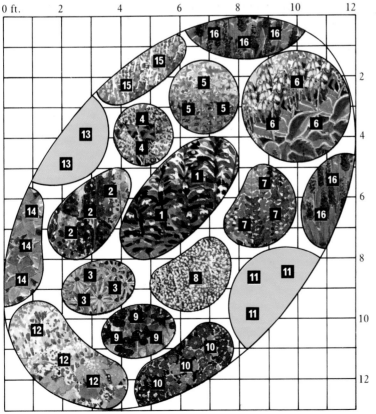

Above Perennial bed. **Left** Plan for the bed. Colored areas indicate plants in flower in mid summer. Average flowering periods are:

1 *Acanthus:* Mid–late summer **2** *Delphiniums:* Early–mid summer **3** *Rudbeckia:* Mid summer–early autumn **4** *Phlox:* Mid–late summer **5** *Coreopsis:* Early summer–early autumn **6** *Hostas:* Mid summer **7** *Lupines:* Late spring–mid summer **8** *Gypsophila:* Early–mid summer **9** *Geum:* Early–late summer **10** *Helianthemum:* Mid summer **11** *Sedum:* Late summer–mid autumn **12** *Alchemilla:* Early –late summer **13** *Solidago:* Late summer–early autumn **14** *Campanula:* Mid–late summer **15** *Nepeta:* Late spring–late summer **16** *Polygonum:* Late summer

Method

Choose a site where the sun will be directly on the bed for at least half the day, as herbaceous perennials are sun lovers. Start by laying out the bed using a hose (the normal technique using a garden line or four stakes and some string is more difficult to apply to a bed with rounded edges). Unroll the hose and lay it roughly in position.

   Cut the bed out, using the edge of the hose as a guide. Use the spade the wrong way around so that its blade enters the soil at right angles, giving a clean, straight edge that can easily be kept tidy with shears later. Prepare the soil as described in the introduction.

Mid spring

Before planting   Stand the plants, still in pots, in their planting positions. Turn each one so that its best side faces outward.

Planting   Plant from the middle of the bed. Lift each plant in turn, mark its position with a trowel, and knock it out of its pot. A tap on the base with the handle of the trowel will quickly dislodge it. Dig a hole the same size as the pot and fit the plant's rootball into it.

   Check that the best side is still facing outward and that the top of the rootball is level with the surface of the surrounding soil before filling in around the roots with soil. Firm each plant gently in place with the handle of the trowel. Scuff out the footprints you make with the point of the trowel.

   When all the plants are in, give the whole bed a thorough watering using the hose – a lawn sprinkler makes this job very much quicker. Then spread a 'mulch' of leaf mold, garden compost or bark chips all over the surface of the bed. This is not strictly essential, but it is beneficial to the plants.

   If slugs are a problem in your garden set out baited slug traps, following the manufacturer's directions.

Late spring

MAINTENANCE

In the first few weeks after planting check weekly to see if watering is required and, if so, use the hose or lawn sprinkler again to give the bed a thorough soaking.

   Hand weed the entire perennial bed every 2 weeks to ensure that the plants are not smothered by weeds, which will inhibit their growth and can restrict flowering. If using a hoe take great care to avoid slicing into the stems of the plants and hoe only very shallowly to avoid cutting into the roots, which grow quite near the surface. Alternatively, use a weedkiller especially formulated for use among flowers, but take care not to exceed the stated dose or it can retard the growth of your plants.

> **In subsequent years,** feed the bed with 2–3 pounds of fertilizer per 100 square feet as soon as the plants start to show signs of growth. Snap the old flower stems of sedum off at the base.

Push a 7 foot stake in alongside each delphinium, placing it on the side of the plant closest to the middle of the bed where it will be least obtrusive. Hammer the

(Late spring)	stake 18–24 inches into the ground and secure the stem to it with plant ties.

In windy areas, support geum, rudbeckia, gypsophila, lupines and phlox by pushing two twigs or slender stakes 12 inches into the ground beside each plant.

Weed every 2 weeks, as in mid spring.

If you are using slug traps, check them often. Empty them and replenish bait as necessary. |
| **Early summer** | Continue tying the growing flower stems of delphiniums to their stakes to ensure the flowers are properly supported when they open.

Check slug traps frequently. Continue weeding. |
| **Mid summer** | Tie the flower stems of delphinium to stakes for the first few weeks. When the flowers are over, take the dead heads off partway down the stem, cutting just above a healthy-looking leaf. Do the same with lupines. Cut the dead flower heads regularly from all the plants as soon as they are over to encourage them to keep producing new blooms. Continue to check slug traps. |
| **Late summer** | Cut helianthemum to within 6 inches of ground level. Remove dead flower stems and foliage from polygonum.

Replenish slug bait if necessary, and continue weeding. |
| **Early autumn** | Cut the flower stems and leaves of hosta, delphinium, lupine, gypsophila, nepeta, geum and acanthus right down to ground level and remove and burn them. Cut back coreopsis after flowering. Remove the stems and old foliage of alchemilla. Deadhead rudbeckia as flowers fade. |
| **Mid autumn** | Do not remove the stems of sedum, as they are needed to give some protection to the developing young shoots early next spring.

Remove debris from the bed and leave it tidy for winter. |
| **Late autumn** | Cut rudbeckia and solidago stems to the ground. |

Blue and White

*Here the basic plan has been adapted to create a fashionable new look
– a 'monochromatic' color scheme of blue and white flowers only.
Buy the following plants to replace those shown in brackets.*

Mid spring

2 *Chrysanthemum maximum* (Shasta daisy)
(replace *Rudbeckia fulgida* 'Goldsturm')

2 *Phlox paniculata* 'White Admiral'
(replace *Phlox paniculata* 'Marlborough')

4 *Campanula medium* 'Calycanthema'
(replace *Coreopsis verticillata*)

4 *Lilium candidum* (lilies) (replace *Lupinus*
'Russell Hybrids')

2 *Salvia* × *superba* (replace *Geum
chiloense* 'Mrs. Bradshaw')

6 *Ajuga reptans* (replace *Helianthemum
nummularium*)

4 *Nepeta* × *faassenii* (replace *Sedum
spectabile* 'Autumn Joy')

3 *Liriope muscari* (replace *Sedum spectabile*
'Autumn Joy')

5 *Anaphalis triplinervis* (replace *Alchemilla
mollis*, *Campanula carpatica* 'Jingle Bells'
and 2 *Polygonum affine*)

2 *Geranium* 'Johnson's Blue' (replace
Solidago 'Golden Sun')

6 *Dianthus* 'Blanche' (replace 3 *Polygonum
affine*)

From the garden shed

1 × 2 gallon bucketful peat

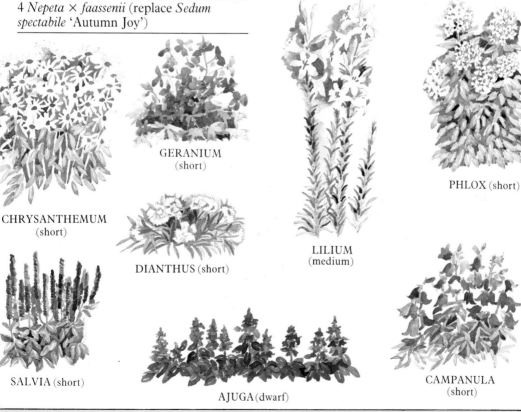

GERANIUM
(short)

CHRYSANTHEMUM
(short)

DIANTHUS (short)

LILIUM
(medium)

PHLOX (short)

SALVIA (short)

AJUGA (dwarf)

CAMPANULA
(short)

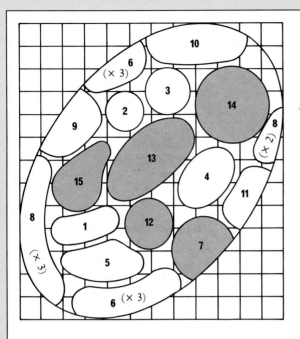

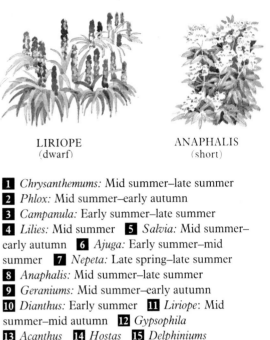

LIRIOPE
(dwarf)

ANAPHALIS
(short)

1 *Chrysanthemums:* Mid summer–late summer
2 *Phlox:* Mid summer–early autumn
3 *Campanula:* Early summer–late summer
4 *Lilies:* Mid summer   **5** *Salvia:* Mid summer–
early autumn   **6** *Ajuga:* Early summer–mid
summer   **7** *Nepeta:* Late spring–late summer
8 *Anaphalis:* Mid summer–late summer
9 *Geraniums:* Mid summer–early autumn
10 *Dianthus:* Early summer   **11** *Liriope*: Mid
summer–mid autumn   **12** *Gypsophila*
13 *Acanthus*   **14** *Hostas*   **15** *Delphiniums*

Mid spring   Prepare the bed as
described on page 29. Plant all plants
except lilies, as described on page 29.

Early summer   Cut off the dead flower stems of dianthus completely as soon as they are over.

Mid summer   Start regularly deadheading salvia every 2
weeks. Cut the flower stem back as far as a healthy leaf.
Remove dead heads from ajuga after flowering by clipping lightly over plants with shears.

Late summer   Cut some of the stems of anaphalis to dry
as "everlasting" flowers. Deadhead salvia every 2 weeks.

Early autumn   Cut the stems of anaphalis, chrysanthemum and phlox back almost to ground level. Pull out
campanula when flowers are finished. Cut down dead
flower stems and foliage on nepeta. Cut off the dead
flower heads of geranium.

Mid autumn   Plant the lilies. Dig a
hole slightly larger than the bulb, place
a handful of peat at the bottom and
press the bulb firmly into this with a
slight screwing motion. Fill the holes
with soil, leaving the tip of each bulb
showing just above the surface.

Late autumn   Cut down the flower spikes of liriope.

Pink and Silver

This variation gives another monochromatic theme, this time in pink and silver. Buy the following plants to replace those shown in brackets.

Mid spring

3 *Monarda didyma* 'Croftway Pink' (replace *Delphinium* 'Pacific Hybrids')

2 *Chrysanthemum maximum* (replace *Rudbeckia fulgida* 'Goldsturm')

2 *Phlox paniculata* 'Eva Cullum' (replace *Phlox paniculata* 'Marlborough')

2 *Astrantia major* (replace *Coreopsis verticillata*)

3 *Chrysanthemum coccineum* 'Eileen May Robinson' (replace *Lupinus* 'Russell Hybrids')

3 *Heuchera sanguinea* (replace *Geum chiloense* 'Mrs. Bradshaw')

3 *Stachys lanata* (replace *Helianthemum nummularium*)

3 *Armeria maritima* (replace *Sedum spectabile* 'Autumn Joy')

2 *Bergenia cordifolia* (replace *Alchemilla mollis*)

2 *Geranium endressii* 'Wargrave Pink' (replace *Solidago* 'Golden Sun')

3 *Anaphalis triplinervis* (replace *Campanula carpatica* 'Jingle Bells')

3 *Stachys lanata* (replace *Nepeta* × *faassenii*)

6 *Dianthus* 'Doris' and 2 *Anaphalis triplinervis* (replace *Polygonum affine*)

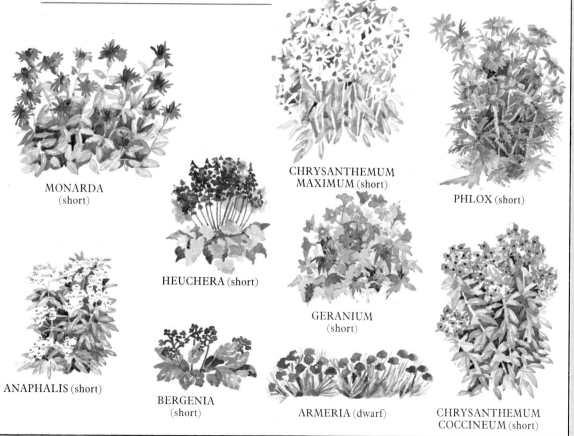

MONARDA (short)

CHRYSANTHEMUM MAXIMUM (short)

PHLOX (short)

HEUCHERA (short)

GERANIUM (short)

ANAPHALIS (short)

BERGENIA (short)

ARMERIA (dwarf)

CHRYSANTHEMUM COCCINEUM (short)

Mid spring Prepare and plant the bed as described on page 29, using the plants listed here.

ASTRANTIA (short)

DIANTHUS (short)

STACHYS (dwarf)

1 *Monarda*: Early–late summer
2 *Chrysanthemum maximum*: Early–late summer **3** *Phlox*: Mid–late summer
4 *Astrantia*: Early–mid summer
5 *Chrysanthemum coccineum*: Early–mid summer **6** *Heuchera*: Early–late summer
7 *Stachys*: Mid summer **8** *Armeria*: Spring–mid summer **9** *Bergenia*: Spring
10 *Geraniums*: Spring–late summer
11 *Anaphalis*: Mid–late summer
12 *Dianthus*: Early–mid summer
13 *Gypsophila* **14** *Acanthus* **15** *Hostas*

Late spring In windy areas, push some $2\frac{1}{2}$ foot tall twigs or slender stakes into the soil around astrantia and *Chrysanthemum coccineum*.

Early summer Snip off the dead flower heads from dianthus and bergenia as soon as they are over.

Mid summer Continue deadheading dianthus, and bergenia.
Cut back the flower stems of *Chrysanthemum coccineum* to encourage a second flush of flowers later.

Late summer Snip the dead flower stems from armeria.

Mid autumn Cut the stems of anaphalis, astrantia, monarda, geranium, phlox and *Chrysanthemum maximum* down almost to ground level. Remove the flower stems only of heuchera and stachys, leaving the foliage.
Select straggly or broken dianthus shoots and cut back to their base using pruning shears.

In subsequent years, you may find heuchera plants have grown so that their crowns are raised slightly above the level of the surrounding soil. If this happens, tuck a handful or two of peat or garden compost under and around them.

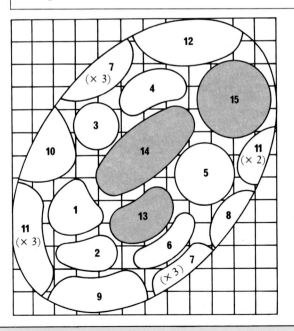

For an 18 foot × 13 foot Bed

This is a longer version of the basic plan, suitable for a larger garden. The shape of the bed and the planting plan are much the same, except that extra plants have been added to elongate the bed. You will not need geum, but you will need the following extra plants.

Mid spring

2 extra *Lupinus* 'Russell Hybrids' (lupine) (5 altogether)

2 *Bergenia cordifolia*

1 extra *Sedum spectabile* 'Autumn Joy'

3 *Chrysanthemum maximum*

2 *Salvia* × *superba*

4 *Aster novi-belgii* (Michaelmas daisy)

3 *Geranium* 'Johnson's Blue'

2 *Stachys lanata*

STACHYS

CHRYSANTHEMUM (short)

SALVIA
(short)

GERANIUM
(short)

BERGENIA (short)

ASTER (short)

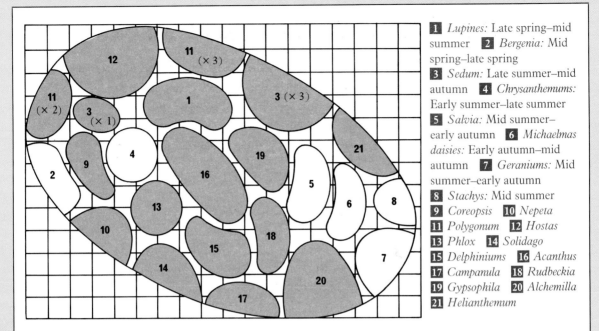

1 *Lupines:* Late spring–mid summer 2 *Bergenia:* Mid spring–late spring
3 *Sedum:* Late summer–mid autumn 4 *Chrysanthemums:* Early summer–late summer
5 *Salvia:* Mid summer–early autumn 6 *Michaelmas daisies:* Early autumn–mid autumn 7 *Geraniums:* Mid summer–early autumn
8 *Stachys:* Mid summer 9 *Coreopsis* 10 *Nepeta* 11 *Polygonum* 12 *Hostas* 13 *Phlox* 14 *Solidago* 15 *Delphiniums* 16 *Acanthus* 17 *Campanula* 18 *Rudbeckia* 19 *Gypsophila* 20 *Alchemilla* 21 *Helianthemum*

Mid spring Prepare and plant the bed as described on page 29, adding the extra plants listed here.

Late spring Push $2\frac{1}{2}$ foot tall twigs or slender stakes into the soil around the asters to give the plants some support.

Throughout summer Snip off the dead flower heads of bergenia, and from then on remove the deadheads from any flowers in the bed as they die as a matter of routine.

Early autumn Cut the stems of geranium and chrysanthemum, and the leaves of bergenia, down to ground level.

Deadhead salvia after flowering is finished.

Remove the flower stems only of stachys, leaving the foliage.

Mid autumn When all the flowers of aster are finished, cut the stems down to ground level.

Replacement and additional plants are given at the start of each variation. For quantities of original plants, uncolored in the planting plan and not given in the variation ingredients, check with the list at the start of the main plan.

In subsequent years, in **early spring**, dig up clumps of aster and divide them, using two garden forks placed back to back to lever them apart. Select healthy pieces from the outside of the clump to replant, and repeat this process annually or the plants will deteriorate.

Every 3–4 years, dig up and divide stachys, chrysanthemum and bergenia.

Beside a Wall, Hedge or Fence

For gardens without room for an island bed, or where a more traditional perennial border is called for, try this final variation. You do not need to buy hosta, geum or solidago.

Mid spring

1 *Acanthus mollis* (replaces 2)

2 *Polygonum affine* (replace 5)

2 *Sedum spectabile* 'Autumn Joy' (replace 3)

2 *Coreopsis verticillata* (replace 3)

From the garden shed

An extra bundle of 2½ foot tall twigs or slender stakes

Garden line

Mid spring Prepare and plant the bed as on page 29, following the plan below.

Immediately after planting the border, be sure to set out baited slug traps if slugs are a problem in your garden.

If the border is directly in front of a hedge, trim the hedge when the border is planted as it will be difficult to do when the flowers have grown up later.

Late spring Push twigs or slender stakes in around all of the plants in the back row of the border (except the delphiniums, which should have stakes put in beside them). In windy areas push sticks in around the plants in the middle row as well.

Throughout summer Water regularly.

Mid autumn After the perennial bed has been cleared of most of its foliage, clean out any weeds and rubbish from the bottom of the hedge behind it and trim it – or do any repairs necessary to the fence or wall, whichever is appropriate. Apply preservative to a fence, using a brand known to be non-toxic to plants rather than creosote.

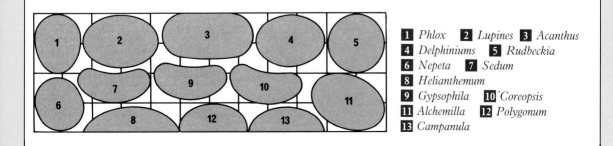

1 *Phlox*	**2** *Lupines*	**3** *Acanthus*
4 *Delphiniums*	**5** *Rudbeckia*	
6 *Nepeta*	**7** *Sedum*	
8 *Helianthemum*		
9 *Gypsophila*	**10** *Coreopsis*	
11 *Alchemilla*	**12** *Polygonum*	
13 *Campanula*		

Herb Gardens

Herbs not only play a valuable role in the kitchen, they add a heady fragrance to the garden. Small but formal, this design contains a selection of herbs chosen for foliage and flower display as well as for culinary use. They are arranged round a centerpiece, which adds a focal point to the design.

Ingredients for a herb garden 6 foot × 6 foot

Mid to late spring

2 Fennel (*Foeniculum vulgare*)

3 Basil (*Ocimum basilicum*)

2 Sage (*Salvia officinalis*)

3 Chives (*Allium schoenoprasum*)

3 Dill (*Anethum graveolens*)

3 Sweet marjoram (*Origanum majorana*)

3 Thyme (*Thymus vulgaris*)

5 Golden oregano (*Origanum vulgare* 'Aureum')

2 Parsley (*Petroselinum crispum*)

1 Apple mint (*Mentha rotundifolia*)

1 Spearmint (*Mentha spicata*)

From the garden shed

4 × 2 gallon bucketfuls of coarse gravel

70 engineering bricks

1 sundial

Concrete paving slab and cement (optional)

4 small ornamental terra cotta pots (frost resistant)

4 broken crocks

Peat moss, leaf mold or straw, for winter protection

Tools required

Spade

Garden fork

Rake

Garden line, or 25 foot of twine and four short stakes

Hand trowel

Watering can or hose

Hoe

Pruning shears

Stick or sharp sand

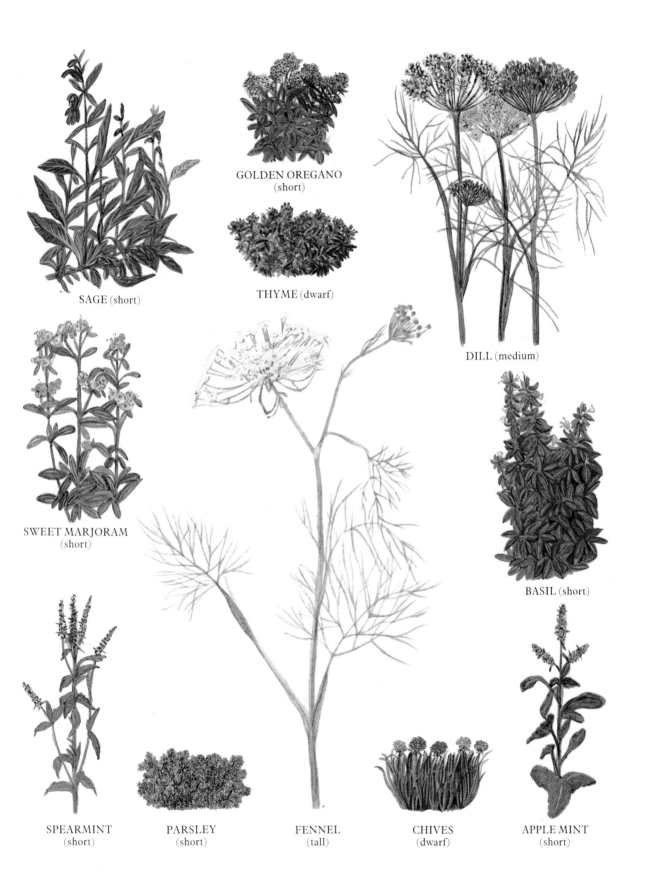

GOLDEN OREGANO
(short)

THYME (dwarf)

SAGE (short)

DILL (medium)

SWEET MARJORAM
(short)

BASIL (short)

SPEARMINT
(short)

PARSLEY
(short)

FENNEL
(tall)

CHIVES
(dwarf)

APPLE MINT
(short)

Method

Choose a sunny but sheltered site and mark out a square 6 foot × 6 foot using a garden line and stakes. Cut alongside the line with the spade. Use the spade the wrong way round so the blade goes into the soil vertically as this gives you a nice clean edge against which to set the border of bricks. Remove the line, and prepare the soil as described in the introduction.

Mark out the shape of the design using the point of a stick or by dribbling sharp sand on to the ground. Lay the engineering bricks round the edge of the garden, and make two brick paths that cross in the center. Set the bricks into the soil firmly, "planting" them with a trowel so that two-thirds of each brick is below the soil surface. Then place the sundial carefully in position in the center of the bed where the two paths cross. If it is a little unsteady you can stand it on a concrete paving slab instead of bricks, anchoring it in place with a dab of cement. Spread a bucketful of coarse gravel in each of the four quarter-circles at the center of the design, where the paths meet.

Mid to late spring

Planting Plant the parsley and the mint in the terra cotta pots. Stand the plants, in their original container, in the ornamental pots to check for size. Put a piece of broken crock over the drainage hole of each pot, followed by sufficient soil to raise the rootball to about 1 inch below the level of the rim. Knock the plants out of their containers by tapping them on the base with a trowel and repot them, filling in with soil as necessary. Stand them on the gravel near the sundial in the center.

Now check with the plan and stand the fennel, basil, sage, chives, dill, thyme, sweet marjoram and golden oregano in position, still in their pots, where they are to be planted. Make sure that they are the right distances apart, and turn each one so that its best side faces outwards in the direction it will normally be seen from.

MAINTENANCE
Herbs are very slow growing, particularly during their first year, and need a certain amount of attention to help them become successfully established. For the first few weeks after planting, always water them during dry weather.

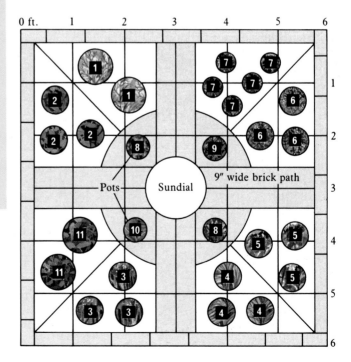

Above opposite Herb garden. **Right** Plan for the herb garden. **1** *Fennel* **2** *Basil* **3** *Chives* **4** *Dill* **5** *Sweet marjoram* **6** *Thyme* **7** *Golden oregano* **8** *Parsley* **9** *Apple mint* **10** *Spearmint* **11** *Sage*

Plant from the center of the bed. Lift each pot in turn and mark its position with the trowel. Gently knock it out of its pot by tapping its base with the trowel and dig a hole the same depth as the pot, as marked. Taking care not to break up the ball of roots, place the plant into its hole. Check that its best side is still facing the right way, then use the trowel to fill in around the roots with soil. Firm around the plant with the trowel handle after planting.

When you have planted the whole bed, water in each plant with approximately 1 pint of water. Spread a layer of peat moss or compost 1 inch deep between the plants.

In subsequent years, replant dill, basil and parsley at this time.

Special note
When you have finished planting it is advisable to spread a thin layer of peat moss or well-rotted garden compost between the plants. Mulching, as this is called, has many beneficial effects; it smothers weed seedlings, improves the soil by adding organic matter to it, insulates the roots of the plants from heat in summer and cold in winter and helps to retain moisture in the soil (particularly important in the case of annuals, which are very shallow-rooted). It also provides a pleasingly uniform dark background to the plants. Mulch again every spring as the growing season begins.

Early summer	Hoe or hand weed the garden once a week to prevent any weeds from taking hold.
Mid summer	Pinch out flowers with your thumb and index finger, as soon as they begin to form (you may want to allow dill and fennel to flower so that you can collect the seeds for culinary use). Weed and water and check for aphids.
Early autumn	Pull out the basil and dill as they begin to die. Cut the chives down to ground level and pull out the parsley as the leaves turn yellow. Prune any untidy branches on the thyme and sage back to the main stem. Cut down fennel stems after collecting seed for culinary use.
Late autumn	If you live in a cold area, cover the marjoram and oregano with a protective layer of shredded leaves, leaf mold or straw. The mints will die back in winter and reappear in spring.

> **In subsequent years**, in **early spring**, scatter fertilizer evenly over the bed (optional), and start hoeing out weeds as soon as new growth appears.

Classical

In this variation a more classical look, reminiscent of the English knot gardens of old, is achieved by replacing the border of bricks in the original plan with a low-trimmed box hedge.

Mid to late spring

1 Sage (*Salvia officinalis*)

2 Chives (*Allium schoenoprasum*)

2 Sweet marjoram (*Origanum majorana*)

2 Dill (*Anethum graveolens*)

3 Thyme (*Thymus vulgaris*)

1 Apple mint (*Mentha rotundifolia*)

4 Parsley (*Petroselinum crispum*)

2 Basil (*Ocimum basilicum*)

100 trained *Buxus sempervirens var. suffruticosa* (box) plants 4 inches wide for edging (if unobtainable already trained, buy small bushy young plants and train your own).

From the garden shed

Hedging shears

Large plastic bag or old bucket

34 engineering bricks for path

Mid to late spring   Plant the sage, chives, sweet marjoram, dill, thyme, parsley and basil following the instructions for sage etc on page 40.

Plant the apple mint. Dig a hole deep enough and wide enough to take the mint's roots, and line with a plastic bag. Fill the bag with soil, and plant the mint in it, following instructions for sage etc on page 40. This prevents the roots from spreading. Alternatively, dig a hole big enough to hold an old bucket, fill the bucket with soil and plant the apple mint in this container.

Plant box hedging in place of the brick boundary and around the outline of the beds, following the instructions for sage etc on page 40. Space the plants 6 inches apart.

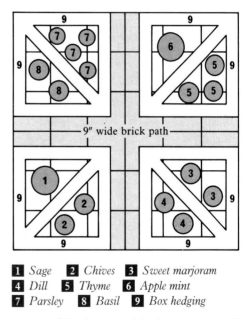

1 Sage	**2** Chives	**3** *Sweet marjoram*
4 *Dill*	**5** *Thyme*	**6** *Apple mint*
7 *Parsley*	**8** *Basil*	**9** *Box hedging*

Mid summer   Clip the box with shears every 6–8 weeks to gradually form the shape of the hedge. Subsequently clip as often as necessary to keep it tidy, and about 4 inches wide and 1 foot high.

BUXUS

Decorative

In this variation herbs have been chosen primarily for their ornamental rather than culinary value; many of them can, nevertheless, be used in certain recipes. The general effect creates a picturesque cottage-style herb garden full of old world charm. The space occupied by the bordering lavender hedge means that fewer plants are required to fill the central beds. You will not need the coarse gravel, boundary bricks or small terra cotta pots.

Early spring

1 Angelica (*Angelica archangelica*)

1 Rue (*Ruta graveolens* 'Jackman's Blue')

15 Dwarf lavender (*Lavandula spica* 'Hidcote')

Late spring

1 Bay tree (*Laurus nobilis*), trained as a standard

3 Parsley (*Petroselinum crispum*)

2 Chives (*Allium schoenoprasum*)

1 Sweet cicely (*Myrrhis odorata*)

1 Sage (*Salvia officinalis*)

1 Fennel (*Foeniculum vulgare*)

2 Sweet marjoram (*Origanum majorana*)

From the garden shed

Hedging shears

38 engineering bricks

Large ornamental terra cotta pot or wooden tub

Bag of potting medium

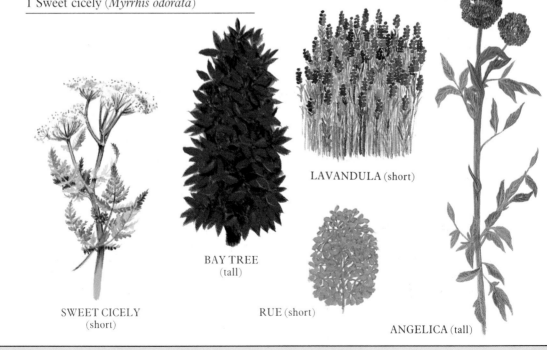

LAVANDULA (short)

BAY TREE
(tall)

SWEET CICELY
(short)

RUE (short)

ANGELICA (tall)

Follow the method described in the original plan for laying the brick paths, but add an extra two bricks to two of the central corners where the paths cross.

Early spring   Plant the lavender hedge following the instructions for sage etc on page 40, spacing the plants 10 inches apart. Plant out the angelica and rue following the instructions for sage etc on page 40.

> **In subsequent years**, replant the angelica every second year.

Late spring   Plant out the parsley, chives, sweet cicely, sage, fennel and sweet marjoram following the instructions for sage etc on page 40.
   Cover the drainage hole of the ornamental pot with crocks and add some potting medium. Knock the container of the bay tree against a hard surface and lift the tree out carefully. Repot in the ornamental container, filling with soil as necessary. Position the tree in the center of the garden.

> **In subsequent years**, replant the parsley at this time.

> Replacement and additional plants are given at the start of each variation. For quantities of original plants, uncolored in the planting plan and not given in the variation ingredients, check with the list at the start of the main plan.

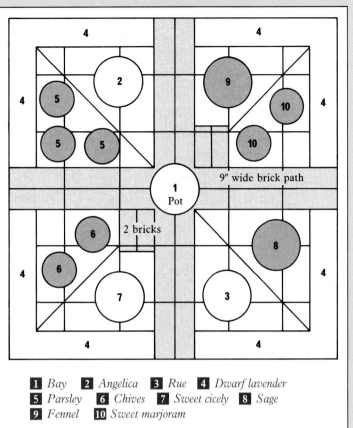

1 Bay   **2** Angelica   **3** Rue   **4** Dwarf lavender
5 Parsley   **6** Chives   **7** Sweet cicely   **8** Sage
9 Fennel   **10** Sweet marjoram

Early autumn   Trim the lavender hedge into shape using hedging shears; this will also be sufficient to remove the dead flower heads. Move the bay tree to a very sheltered place for the winter – a cold greenhouse or porch is ideal. Remove dead flower heads from rue.

> **In subsequent years**, in **mid spring**, trim the rue back to old (darker) wood to keep the plant's bushy shape.
>   In **early autumn**, as the lavender plants become more mature, take care not to cut back into the old, dark-colored wood near the base of the plants. Instead, just clip the soft shoots of the current season's growth. Check the bay tree each year to see if it needs transplanting to a larger pot.

Herb Border

A selection of ornamental and culinary herbs from the previous designs, together with a few new varieties, create an attractive and productive garden bed measuring 15 foot × 4 foot. It is suitable for a sunny situation bordering a wall, fence or hedge. You will not need bricks, ornamental pots or gravel, but you will need more compost or manure, sharp sand and fertilizer.

Early spring

2 Dwarf lavender (*Lavandula spica* 'Hidcote')

1 Chamomile (*Anthemis tinctoria*)

1 Angelica (*Angelica archangelica*)

1 Rue (*Ruta graveolens* 'Jackman's Blue')

1 Rosemary (*Rosmarinus officinalis*)

1 French sorrel (*Rumex scutatus*)

Late spring

1 Bay tree (*Laurus nobilis*), trained as a standard

1 Apple mint (*Mentha rotundifolia*)

1 Thyme (*Thymus vulgaris*)

4 Chives (*Allium schoenoprasum*)

3 Basil (*Ocimum basilicum* 'Dark Opal')

3 Basil (*Ocimum basilicum*)

1 Sage (*Salvia officinalis*)

3 Dill (*Anethum graveolens*)

5 Parsley (*Petroselinum crispum*)

3 Sweet cicely (*Myrrhis odorata*)

1 Sage (*Salvia officinalis* 'Tricolor')

5 Nasturtiums (*Tropaeolum majus*)

3 Golden oregano (*Origanum vulgare* 'Aureum')

From the garden shed

15 × 2 gallon bucketfuls peat moss, well-rotted manure or garden compost

6–7 × 2 gallon bucketfuls sharp sand or gravel (for clay soil)

6 ounces 5–10–5 or other all-purpose fertilizer

5 slender stakes 6 foot high

Large plastic bag or an old bucket

Lawn shears

LAVENDER (short)

SAGE 'Tricolor' (short)

NASTURTIUM (tall)

ROSEMARY (medium)

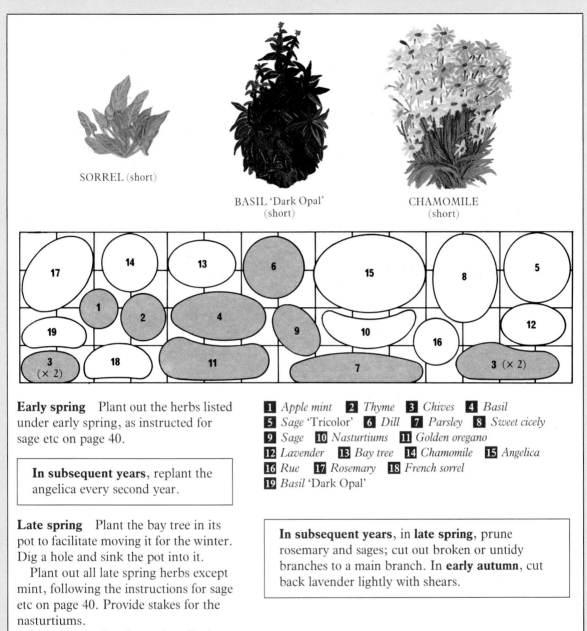

SORREL (short)

BASIL 'Dark Opal'
(short)

CHAMOMILE
(short)

Early spring Plant out the herbs listed under early spring, as instructed for sage etc on page 40.

> **In subsequent years**, replant the angelica every second year.

Late spring Plant the bay tree in its pot to facilitate moving it for the winter. Dig a hole and sink the pot into it.

Plant out all late spring herbs except mint, following the instructions for sage etc on page 40. Provide stakes for the nasturtiums.

Plant the apple mint as described on page 43 to prevent the roots from becoming too invasive.

1 *Apple mint*   **2** *Thyme*   **3** *Chives*   **4** *Basil*
5 *Sage* 'Tricolor'   **6** *Dill*   **7** *Parsley*   **8** *Sweet cicely*
9 *Sage*   **10** *Nasturtiums*   **11** *Golden oregano*
12 *Lavender*   **13** *Bay tree*   **14** *Chamomile*   **15** *Angelica*
16 *Rue*   **17** *Rosemary*   **18** *French sorrel*
19 *Basil* 'Dark Opal'

> **In subsequent years**, in **late spring**, prune rosemary and sages; cut out broken or untidy branches to a main branch. In **early autumn**, cut back lavender lightly with shears.

Early to late summer Pinch out flowering stems of sorrel as they appear.

Early autumn Pull out the nasturtiums and basils as they begin to die.

Mid autumn Cut down old flower stems of chamomile.

Herb Containers

Herbs in containers can be fitted into the tiniest of gardens, using any hardstanding area in a reasonably sheltered sunny location. You need no soil improvers or fertilizer. Use only the following plants:

Late spring

1 Bay tree (*Laurus nobilis*), trained as a standard

1 Sage (*Salvia officinalis*)

1 Parsley (*Petroselinum crispum*)

1 Basil (*Ocimum basilicum*)

1 Spearmint (*Mentha rotundifolia*)

1 Sweet marjoram (*Origanum majorana*)

1 Chives (*Allium schoenoprasum*)

1 Thyme (*Thymus vulgaris*)

From the garden shed

1 windowbox measuring 3 foot × 9 inches

1 × 18 inch diameter terra cotta pot

2 × 9 inch diameter terra cotta pots

2 × 5 inch diameter terra cotta pots (all frost resistant and with drainage holes)

1 large bag of potting medium

Liquid houseplant fertilizer

Stiff brush for cleaning pots

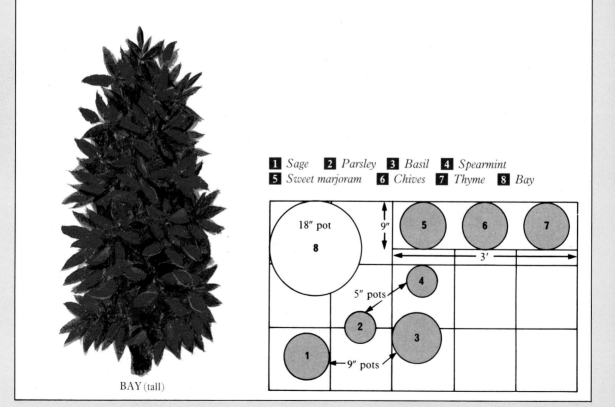

BAY (tall)

1 *Sage* **2** *Parsley* **3** *Basil* **4** *Spearmint*
5 *Sweet marjoram* **6** *Chives* **7** *Thyme* **8** *Bay*

Late spring Repot the bay tree into the 18 inch diameter pot. Cover the drainage hole with old crock and add potting medium. Knock the bay tree container against a hard surface and lift the tree out carefully. Stand in the new pot, fill in with potting medium and firm down.

Secure the windowbox in place. Stand the pots in position and half fill all the containers with potting medium. Knock the herbs out of their pots and place the mint and sage in the center of the 9 inch pots and the parsley and basil in the center of the 5 inch pots. Stand the marjoram, chives and thyme in a row along the center of the windowbox. Then fill around the edges with more potting medium, finishing with the surface of the rootball level with the surface of the potting medium. Firm the potting medium down slightly with your fingers, and water each plant in: about 1 pint of water for each of the smaller pots, 2 pints for the large ones and 3 pints for the windowbox.

> **In subsequent years**, replant new parsley and basil plants.

Check every day to see if more water is needed. You can test very easily by sticking your finger into the potting medium or, alternatively, buy a water meter. Take care not to overwater herbs grown in containers – the potting medium should almost dry out between waterings. In rainy weather watering may not be needed for some time, but during hot dry spells you may need to water every day.

> **In subsequent years**, clean the outside of the pots when necessary with a stiff brush and warm water, adding a little liquid detergent if need be to remove stubborn grime. Take care not to get any inside the pots.

Mid summer Give plants a liquid plant feed once a week.

Early autumn As plant growth slows down, discontinue fertilizing and restrict the amount of water. Basil and parsley can be thrown away after they stop producing usable leaves, and the old leaves of the chives should be cut down when they die back. The containers can remain where they are for the winter, provided they are not standing under drips or in puddles of water.

Winter It is necessary to prevent the roots of plants in containers from freezing in very severe weather. The pots can be insulated by wrapping them in newspaper or cheesecloth, but if a sheltered porch or cold greenhouse is available, they are best moved inside for the very worst of the winter. Bay should always be moved under cover. A shed or garage is better than nothing – but do not leave plants there too long or they will soon suffer from the lack of light.

Old-Fashioned Borders

The old world charm of cottage gardens is back in vogue, and this chapter looks at the elements that make up such a garden – 'old-fashioned' scented roses, aromatic and traditional varieties of flowering plants. The main plan is for a 'classic' old-fashioned border containing a little of everything.

Ingredients for a border 10 foot × 4 foot

Mid spring

1 *Rosa* 'Madame Isaac Pereire' (Bourbon)
1 *Clematis montana*
3 *Verbascum bombyciferum* 'Silver Lining'
2 *Geranium* 'Johnson's Blue'
1 *Geranium endressii* 'Wargrave Pink'
3 *Aster novi-belgii* (Michaelmas daisy)
3 *Campanula medium* (Canterbury bells)
3 *Althaea rosea* (hollyhock)
5 *Lathyrus odoratus* 'Antique Fantasy Mixed' (sweet peas)
3 *Lupinus* 'Russell Hybrids' (lupines)
1 *Alchemilla mollis*
4 *Dianthus* 'Spring Beauty', Mixed Colors
3 *Delphinium* 'Pacific Hybrids'

From the garden shed

Slug traps and bait, if necessary
10 × 2 gallon bucketfuls of garden compost or well-rotted manure for mulching (optional)
6 × 7 foot plant stakes
Plant ties
Bundle of $2\frac{1}{2}$ foot tall slender stakes
Rose insecticide, rose fungicide

Tools required

Spade
Garden fork
Rake
Garden line
Hand trowel
Watering can or hose
Pruning shears
Hoe

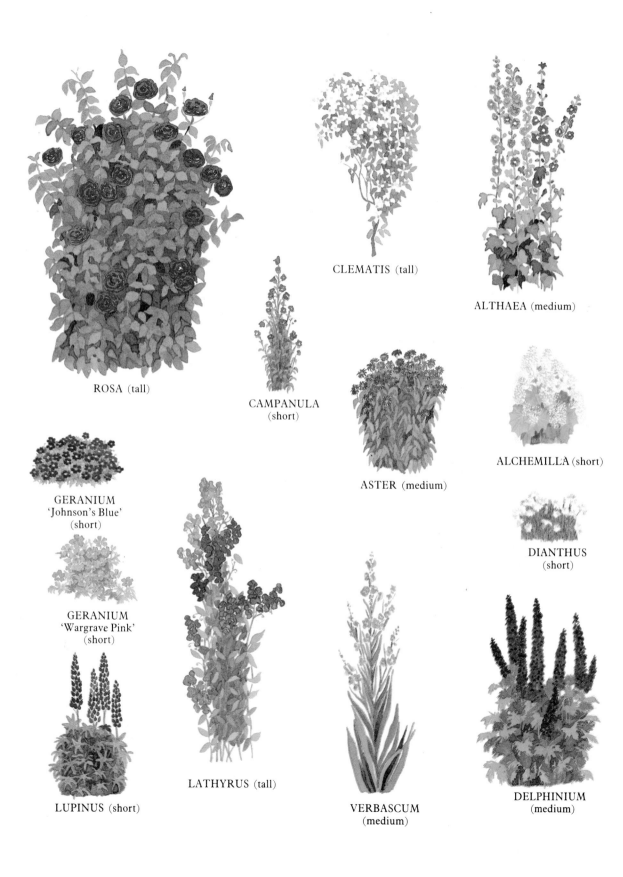

ROSA (tall)

CLEMATIS (tall)

ALTHAEA (medium)

CAMPANULA
(short)

ASTER (medium)

ALCHEMILLA (short)

GERANIUM
'Johnson's Blue'
(short)

DIANTHUS
(short)

GERANIUM
'Wargrave Pink'
(short)

LATHYRUS (tall)

VERBASCUM
(medium)

DELPHINIUM
(medium)

LUPINUS (short)

Method

Choose a site where the sun will shine directly on to the bed for at least half the day. A border such as this would traditionally be in front of a wall or a fence, with a lawn or path bordering it. However, it could also be cut into a lawn near the rear of the property and given an "artificial" back by putting up a series of posts supporting wires, trellis or plastic-covered wire netting on to which the clematis and rose could be trained later.

Lay out the shape of the bed with a garden line or four stakes and a ball of string. If the bed is in a lawn, cut around the edge of the bed using a spade the wrong way around to get a nice vertical edge. This will then be easy to keep tidy by trimming with lawn shears later. Prepare the soil as described in the introduction.

Mid spring

Before planting   Prune the rose 'Madame Isaac Pereire'. To do this, cut the thickest stems down to 12 inches above the top of the pot, and the thinner shoots to 4 inches. Cut out any very spindly, dead or damaged shoots entirely.

Water all the plants thoroughly 12 hours or so before planting.

Stand the plants, still in pots, in their planting positions. Turn each plant so that its best side faces outward, toward the front of the bed.

Planting   Plant from the back of the bed. Lift each plant in turn and mark its position with a trowel. Then, using the pot as a guide, dig a hole the same size as the pot so that the rim is level with the surface of the surrounding soil.

Now knock the plant out of its container. If it is a rigid one, a sharp tap on the base with the handle of the trowel will quickly dislodge it.

If it is a flexible plastic container, cut it away without breaking up the ball of roots inside.

Set the plant into the hole you have made, check that its best side is still facing outward and that the top of the rootball is level with the surface of the soil. Then fill in around the roots with soil. Firm each plant gently in place with the handle of the trowel.

As you plant, scuff out footprints.

MAINTENANCE

Mulch the bed by spreading a thin layer of well-rotted manure or garden compost all over the surface. This is not essential, but it is beneficial to the plants.

If slugs are a problem in your garden, set out baited slug traps, following the manufacturer's directions.

Check weekly to see if watering is required.

Weed the bed every 2 weeks to ensure the plants are not smothered by weeds, which would inhibit their growth and flowering. If you are using a hoe take great care to avoid slicing into the stems of the plants – at this stage, they may not recover from such injury – and hoe very shallowly to avoid cutting into the roots.

In subsequent years, dig up and divide geranium plants and Michaelmas daisies when they get too big, replanting them in the same place as previously. Use two garden forks, back to back, to lever the clump apart. Replant only the best pieces with lots of young growth from around the outside of the clump.

Fertilize the bed with 5–10–5 or other all-purpose fertilizer as soon as the plants start to show signs of growth. Set out baited slug traps if slugs are a problem in your garden.

Control weeds. Mulch around clematis by spreading a bucketful of compost evenly over its roots to help keep them moist during the summer.

Keep the new plants well watered for the first 6–8 weeks after planting and check them subsequently during dry spells. Established plants are unlikely to need watering except in prolonged droughts.

Above Old-fashioned border. **Below** Planting plan. Colored areas indicate plants in flower in mid summer. Average flowering periods are listed below: **1** *Bourbon rose*: Early summer–late summer, early–mid autumn **2** *Clematis*: Late spring **3** *Verbascum*: Early–late summer **4** *Geranium* 'Johnson's Blue': Late spring–early autumn **5** *Geranium* 'Wargrave Pink': Late spring–late summer **6** *Michaelmas daisies*: Late summer–mid autumn **7** *Campanula*: Early–mid summer **8** *Hollyhocks*: Mid–late summer **9** *Sweet peas*: Early summer–early autumn **10** *Lupines*: Late spring–mid summer **11** *Alchemilla*: Early–late summer **12** *Dianthus*: Early–mid summer **13** *Delphiniums*: Early–mid summer

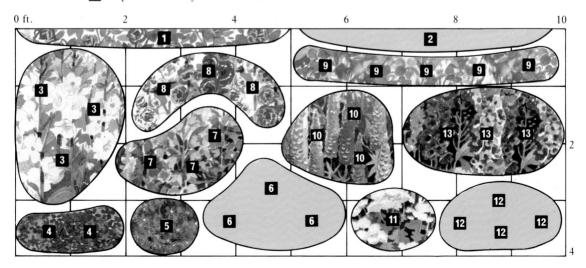

Water the plants once they are all in, giving each one about 1 pint of water, apart from the rose and clematis, which should have 1 gallon each. Use a watering can or hose and, if the soil is very dry, soak the entire bed.

> **In subsequent years**, plant new verbascum, sweet peas and campanula.

Late spring

Support delphiniums and hollyhocks by pushing a 7 foot stake in behind each plant, where it will be least obtrusive. Hammer the stake 18–24 inches into the ground and secure the stem to it with plant ties.

Support sweet peas by pushing two $2\frac{1}{2}$ foot high slender stakes in beside each plant. There is no need to tie them, as sweet peas produce tendrils that cling on to the sticks without help.

In windy areas, provide stakes for lupines and Michaelmas daisies too. These should be pushed 12 inches into the ground.

Check slug traps. Empty them and renew bait as necessary.

Weed the bed every 2 weeks.

Water every week if necessary.

> **In subsequent years**, when the flowers of clematis are over the plant can be pruned to restrict it from growing. Simply shorten the shoots that are too long by the required amount.

Early summer

Tie the clematis to its support as it grows to help it start to climb over the fence or trellis. Encourage it to form a backdrop to the rose.

Tie the developing flower stems of delphiniums to their stakes to ensure the flowers are straight when open.

Spray the rose regularly with an insecticide against aphids and a rose fungicide against blackspot and mildew. Deadhead the rose regularly every week to encourage further flowering, cutting the stem just above the topmost leaf.

Deadhead dianthus when the flowers are over, removing the flower stem completely.

(**Early summer**)	Cut off the dead flower stems from sweet peas throughout the summer to promote the development of new buds and encourage the plants to flower continuously. Continue checking slug traps and weed regularly every 2 weeks.
Mid summer	Deadhead the delphiniums and lupines when the flowers are over. Cut the dead flowers off partway down the stem, just above a healthy-looking leaf. In this way you can sometimes coax the plants to produce a few more flowers. Continue deadheading the rose, and sweet peas. Continue tying in clematis and hollyhocks. Spray rose against aphids, blackspot and mildew.
Late summer	Continue tying the hollyhock flowers to their stakes, and deadheading the sweet peas.
Early autumn **In subsequent years**, spray Michaelmas daisies with a fungicide if they are affected by mildew.	Deadhead the rose, which in a good summer will be producing a second flush of flowers now. Be prepared to start spraying the plant if patches of mildew (which looks like talcum powder) appear on the foliage. Cut down the flower stems and leaves of delphiniums, lupines and geraniums to ground level towards the end of September after they have finished flowering. Cut back the flower stems and old foliage only of alchemilla, when flowering finishes. Pull out campanula, sweet peas, verbascum and hollyhocks after all their flowers are faded. Clear away weeds, stakes, etc.
Mid autumn **In subsequent years**, prune the rose by cutting to ground level all the old, diseased and damaged stems, and any that are overcrowded. Then tie in the young shoots that have grown over the summer, in their place. No other pruning is needed.	Prune the rose as soon as the last flowers are over: cut to ground level the thinnest of the stems that have flowered this summer and tie the new shoots that have grown up over the summer in their place. The remaining stems that flowered should have their sideshoots cut back to within 2–3 leaves of where they join the main stem. If you live where the winters are cold, protect the rose for the winter by pegging the canes to the ground and covering them with an 8–10 inch mound of soil. After the ground freezes later on in autumn or winter, add a 10 inch layer of mulch atop the soil mound. Cut the stems of Michaelmas daisies to ground level after flowering. Remove stakes.

Scented

Any old-fashioned border worthy of its name is faintly aromatic, but this variation contains plants selected especially for their scent. The design is the same as before, but some of the plants have changed to give a garden with an extra dimension. You will not need any stakes or plant ties for this border.

Mid spring

1 *Lonicera japonica* 'Halliana' (honeysuckle) (replaces *Clematis montana*)

4 *Lilium regale* (lily) (replace *Verbascum bombyciferum* 'Silver Lining')

2 *Nepeta* × *faassenii* (replace *Geranium* 'Johnson's Blue')

12 *Malcolmia maritima* or a packet of seed (Virginia stock) (replace *Geranium endressii* 'Wargrave Pink')

1 *Origanum vulgare* 'Aureum' (golden oregano), and
3 *Viola* 'Violet Queen' (pansy)
   (replace *Aster novi-belgii*)

6 *Reseda odorata* (mignonette) (replace *Campanula medium*)

3 *Monarda didyma* 'Croftway Pink' (replace *Lupinus* 'Russell Hybrids')

1 *Lavandula spica* 'Hidcote' (replaces *Alchemilla mollis*)

3 *Hesperis matronalis* (replace *Delphinium* 'Pacific Hybrids')

Late spring

6 *Nicotiana alata* 'Sensation Mixed' (replace *Althaea rosea*)

From the garden shed

Extra stakes

Tools required

Hedging shears

HESPERIS (short)

LAVANDULA (short)

NICOTIANA (short)

RESEDA (short)

LONICERA (medium)

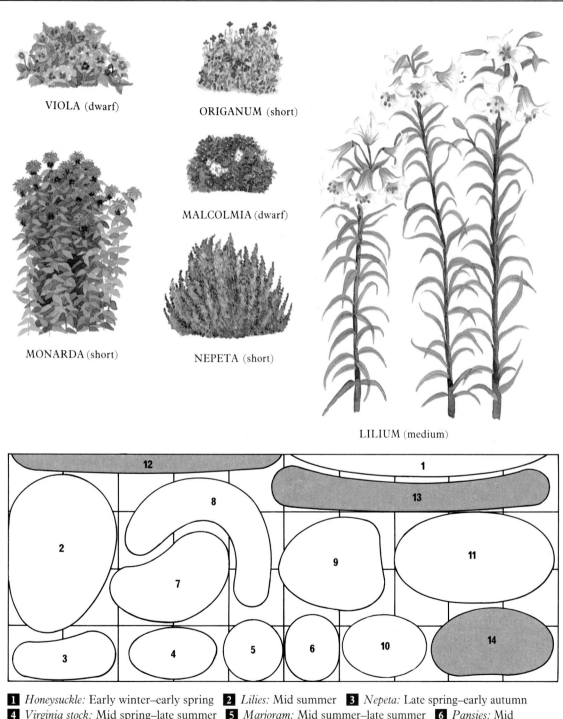

VIOLA (dwarf)

ORIGANUM (short)

MALCOLMIA (dwarf)

MONARDA (short)

NEPETA (short)

LILIUM (medium)

1 *Honeysuckle:* Early winter–early spring **2** *Lilies:* Mid summer **3** *Nepeta:* Late spring–early autumn **4** *Virginia stock:* Mid spring–late summer **5** *Marjoram:* Mid summer–late summer **6** *Pansies:* Mid spring–early summer **7** *Mignonette:* Mid summer–late summer **8** *Nicotiana:* Mid summer–late summer **9** *Monarda:* Early summer–late summer **10** *Lavender:* Early summer–mid summer **11** *Hesperis:* Early summer–mid summer **12** *Bourbon rose* **13** *Sweet peas* **14** *Dianthus*

Mid spring Prepare the bed and plant the honeysuckle, nepeta, Virginia stock, oregano, pansies, mignonette, monarda, lavender and hesperis following the instructions on page 52.

To plant the lily bulbs, dig holes 9 inches deep and sprinkle a little compost at the bottom of the holes. Put a bulb in each, pointed end up, and settle it into the compost with a slight twisting motion. Fill in with soil and firm the soil down with the handle of the trowel.

Sow seeds of Virginia stock if plants are not available. Rake the area to produce a fine tilth, then scatter the seeds thinly and rake over the area lightly to cover the seeds. Water well.

> **In subsequent years**, replant mignonette, Virginia stock and pansies.

Late spring Plant out the nicotiana following the instructions on page 52 after the last danger of frost has passed.

> **In subsequent years**, replant nicotiana.

> Replacement and additional plants are given at the start of each variation. For quantities of original plants, uncolored in the planting plan and not given in the variation ingredients, check with the list at the start of the main plan.

There is no need to thin out the Virginia stock seedlings when they come up, and the plants may start flowering in as little as 4 weeks.

> **In subsequent years**, dig up and divide monarda at the beginning of April. This will need doing every 2–3 years to maintain the vigor of the plants. Divide them by using two garden forks back to back to lever the clump apart. Replant only those pieces with young growth from around the edge of the clump.
>
> Mulch the honeysuckle following the instructions for clematis on page 52.
>
> Mulch between the lilies, taking care not to break off any young shoots.
>
> Prune the honeysuckle if it becomes overgrown or straggly. Simply cut back as required to a maximum of 50 per cent of the size of the plant, always cutting just above the leaf joints. Regular pruning is not necessary.

Support nicotiana and hesperis by pushing stakes in between the plants. In windy areas support the lilies, monarda and mignonette in the same way.

Throughout summer Deadhead the pansies regularly, snipping off the flower stems.

Do not, however, remove the dead flower heads from hesperis and Virginia stock, as the plants will eventually re-seed themselves.

Mid autumn Cut down and remove the dead flower stems and foliage from the lilies, nepeta and monarda.

Pull out Virginia stock, nicotiana, mignonette and pansies as soon as their flowers are finished.

> **In subsequent years**, clip lavender lightly with shears after the flowers are over to remove the dead heads and reshape the plants. Do not prune back into the old, dark-colored wood.
>
> Cut back oregano by about half its height if it is untidy or full of woody stems and dead flower heads. In very cold regions, it will have to be replanted each year.

Traditional

This variation concentrates particularly on species plants, simple flowers and old-fashioned aromatics to give a border with an especially traditional air about it. Buy the following plants, which replace those shown in brackets from our original list.

Mid spring

3 *Lathyrus latifolius* (perennial pea) (replace *Clematis montana* and *Lathyrus odoratus* 'Antique Fantasy Mixed')

1 *extra Alchemilla mollis* (replaces *Geranium endressi* 'Wargrave Pink')

3 *Saxifraga* × *umbrosa* (saxifrage) (replace *Aster novi-belgii*)

2 *Digitalis purpurea* (foxglove) (replace *Althaea rosea*)

2 *Dicentra spectabilis* (replace *Lupinus* 'Russell Hybrids')

3 *Hesperis matronalis* (replace *Delphinium* 'Pacific Hybrids')

1 *Kniphofia uvaria*

HESPERIS
(short)

KNIPHOFIA (short)

SAXIFRAGA (short)

DIGITALIS (medium)

LATHYRUS (tall)

DICENTRA (short)

ALCHEMILLA (short)

Mid spring Prepare the bed and plant following the instructions on page 52.

In subsequent years, plant new foxglove and campanula each year.

Mid spring Support hesperis by pushing stakes in between the plants. In windy areas it is also advisable to support dicentra in the same way.

Train the sweet pea plants up on to the trellis or netting they are to grow up. Put a few slender stakes in front of the plants to encourage them to spread outward across the wall or fence behind them. Once they have started to climb they are entirely self-supporting.

Early summer Deadhead the perennial peas regularly, snipping off the flower stems, and cut them for the house just as you would with annual sweet peas.

Deadhead saxifrage by cutting the flower stems to ground level after the flowers are over.

Mid summer Leave hesperis flower heads to seed.

Deadhead the dicentra by cutting off the flowers, and continue deadheading the perennial peas.

Late summer Continue deadheading the perennial peas as above.

Early autumn Cut down the dead flower stems and old foliage of alchemilla and dicentra. Remove the old flower stems only of kniphofia.

Pull out foxglove plants after the flowers are finished.

Cut down the stems and foliage of perennial peas to ground level when they die.

1 *Perennial sweet peas:* Early summer–early autumn **2** *Alchemilla:* Early summer–late summer **3** *Saxifrage:* Late spring **4** *Foxgloves:* Early summer–mid summer **5** *Dicentra:* Late spring–early summer **6** *Hesperis:* Early summer **7** *Kniphofia:* Mid summer–early autumn **8** *Bourbon rose* **9** *Verbascum* **10** *Geranium* ('Johnson's Blue') **11** *Campanula* **12** *Dianthus*

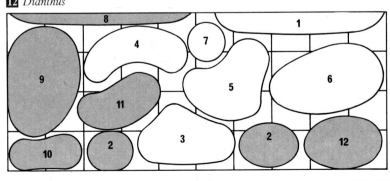

Border for Cut Flowers

One of the great joys of an old-fashioned border is being able to cut flowers for the house. This variation includes plants for flower arranging, for a garden that gives pleasure indoors and out.

Early to mid spring

12 *Lathyrus odoratus* 'Jet Set Mixed' (sweet peas) (replace *Clematis montana*)

4 *Lilium regale* (replace *Verbascum bombyciferum* 'Silver Lining')

1 *Hosta fortunei* 'Albopicta' (replaces *Geranium* 'Johnson's Blue')

3 *Viola* 'Yellow Queen' (pansy) (replace *Geranium endressii* 'Wargrave Pink')

3 *Aster* × *frikartii* (replace *Aster novi-belgii*)

2 *Scabiosa caucasica* (scabious) (replace *Campanula medium*)

2 *Phlox paniculata* 'Eva Cullum' (replace *Lupinus* 'Russell Hybrids')

1 *Lavandula spica* 'Hidcote' (replaces *Alchemilla mollis*)

4 *Dianthus* 'Doris' (modern pink) (replace *Dianthus* 'Spring Beauty')

Late spring

3 *Nicotiana alata* 'Sensation Mixed' (replace *Althaea rosea*)

Tools required

Hedging shears

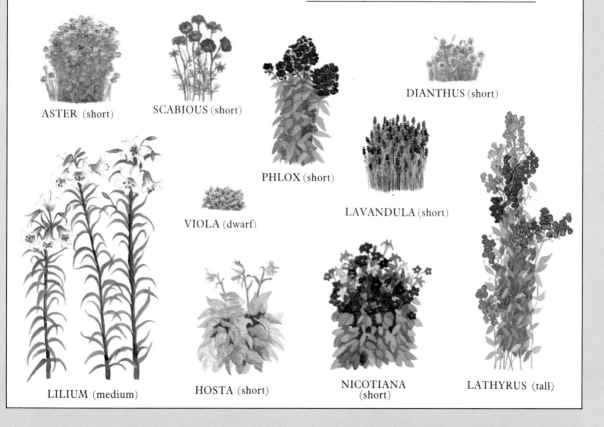

ASTER (short)

SCABIOUS (short)

DIANTHUS (short)

PHLOX (short)

VIOLA (dwarf)

LAVANDULA (short)

LILIUM (medium)

HOSTA (short)

NICOTIANA (short)

LATHYRUS (tall)

Early to mid spring   Plant the sweet peas, hosta, pansies, aster, scabious, phlox, lavender and dianthus following the instructions on page 52.

Plant the lilies following the instructions on page 58.

> **In subsequent years**, replant the pansies and the sweet peas.

Late spring   Plant out nicotiana after the last danger of frost has passed, following the instructions on page 52.

> **In subsequent years**, replant nicotiana.

> **In subsequent years**, mulch between the lilies, taking care not to break off any young shoots.

Support aster and phlox with slender stakes.

Put slender stakes in for some of the sweet peas to grow up. Train one row up the trellis or fence at the back of the bed, the second up the slender stakes.

Early and mid summer   Protect hostas from slugs if necessary by setting out baited traps.

Deadhead pansies and dianthus regularly, snipping off the flower stems, to encourage plenty of new flowers.

Late summer   Continue deadheading pansies, as above, and protecting hostas against slugs.

Early autumn   Cut down phlox and hosta to ground level after the foliage has started to die back naturally. Cut down dead flower stems and foliage from the lilies.

Pull out nicotiana, sweet peas and pansies when the last of the flowers are over.

Clip lavender with shears to remove the dead flowers and reshape the plants. Do not cut into the old, dark-colored wood as this may kill the plant.

> **In subsequent years**, dianthus may need light pruning: cut straggly or broken shoots back to base.

Mid autumn   Cut down scabious to ground level. Remove all debris from the bed and leave it tidy for winter.

1 *Sweet peas:* Early summer– early autumn   **2** *Lilies:* Mid summer   **3** *Hosta:* Mid summer   **4** *Pansies:* Late spring–early autumn   **5** *Asters:* Late summer–mid autumn   **6** *Scabious:* Early summer–early autumn   **7** *Nicotiana:* Early summer– early autumn   **8** *Phlox:* Mid summer–early autumn   **9** *Lavender:* Mid summer– early autumn   **10** *Dianthus:* Early summer   **11** *Bourbon rose* **12** *Delphiniums*

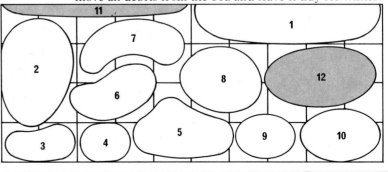

Shady

Not everyone is lucky enough to have a border in a sunny position, so for those who don't the final variation is for an old-fashioned border that will add a dash of color to a shady spot.

Mid spring

2 *Lonicera heckrottii* (honeysuckle) (replaces *Rosa* 'Madame Isaac Pereire' and *Clematis montana*)

4 *Lilium regale* (lily) (replace *Verbascum bombyciferum* 'Silver Lining')

3 *Viola* 'Roggli Giants' (pansy) (replace *Geranium* 'Johnson's Blue')

1 *Alchemilla mollis* (replaces *Geranium endressii* 'Wargrave Pink')

3 *Pulmonaria officinalis*, and
1 *Heuchera sanguinea*
   (replace *Aster novi-belgii*)

1 *Helleborus orientalis* (replaces *Campanula medium*)

3 *Digitalis purpurea* (foxglove) (replace *Althaea rosea*)

1 *Polygonatum multiflorum* (Solomon's seal),
1 *Solidago canadensis*, and
3 *Aquilegia* 'McKana Hybrids' (columbine)
   (replace *Lathyrus odoratus* 'Antique
   Fantasy Mixed')

2 *Hemerocallis* 'Lillian Frye' (replace *Lupinus* 'Russell Hybrids')

2 *Primula vulgaris* (replace *Alchemilla mollis*)

3 *Anemone* × *hybrida* (replace *Delphinium* 'Pacific Hybrids')

Mid autumn

4 *Convallaria majalis* (lily of the valley) (replace *Dianthus* 'Spring Beauty')

AQUILEGIA (short)

PULMONARIA (dwarf)

VIOLA (dwarf)

HELLEBORUS (short)

LILIUM (medium)

HEUCHERA (short)

LONICERA (tall)
'Belgica'

LONICERA (tall)
'Serotina'

HEMEROCALLIS
(short)

PRIMULA
(dwarf)

ANEMONE (short)

CONVALLARIA (dwarf)

SOLIDAGO (short)

POLYGONATUM (short)

DIGITALIS (medium)

Mid spring To plant the lilies, dig holes 9 inches deep and sprinkle a little compost at the bottom of each. Put one bulb in each hole, pointed end up, and settle it into the compost with a slight twisting motion. Fill in with soil and firm it gently with the handle of the trowel.

Plant the honeysuckle, pansies, alchemilla, pulmonaria, heuchera, helleborus, foxglove, Solomon's seal, solidago, columbine, hemerocallis, primula and anemone following the instructions on page 52.

In subsequent years, replant pansies and foxgloves annually.

In subsequent years, prune the honeysuckle if it becomes overgrown or straggly. Cut back as required to a maximum of 50 per cent of the size of the plant, always cutting just above the leaf joints. Regular pruning is not necessary. Deadhead the hellebore and primula after flowering.

Mulch carefully between the lilies, taking care not to break off any of the young shoots just coming through.

Early summer Set out slug traps if necessary and check them often.

Deadhead the pansies every two weeks, snipping off the flower stems, to encourage a constant supply of new flowers to develop. Cut back pulmonaria and lily of the valley flower stems after flowering.

Cut columbine flower stems down to ground level, after flowering.

Cut off heuchera flower stems after flowering.

Mid and late summer Continue checking slug traps, and deadheading pansies.

Early autumn Pull out pansies and foxgloves after the last flowers are over.

Cut down the flower stems and old leaves of alchemilla.

Cut Solomon's seal down to ground level when the leaves start to die off. Cut down and remove flower stems and foliage from the lilies when they die back.

Mid autumn Plant the pips of lily of the valley, pointed ends uppermost, just below the surface of the soil.

Cut down anemone to ground level after flowering is over. Cut solidago flower stems to ground level after flowering.

In subsequent years, dig up and divide anemone and Solomon's seal when the clumps become large. Use two garden forks back to back to lever them apart. Replant the best pieces in the same position as previously.

---

1 *Honeysuckle* ('Serotina'): Early summer–mid autumn
2 *Honeysuckle* ('Belgica'): Late spring–early summer
3 *Lilies*: Early summer
4 *Pansies*: Early summer–early autumn **5** *Alchemilla*: Early–late summer
6 *Pulmonaria*: Mid–late spring **7** *Heuchera*: Early summer
8 *Helleborus*: Late winter– early spring **9** *Foxgloves*: Early–late summer
10 *Solomon's seal*: Early summer **11** *Solidago*: Late summer–early autumn
12 *Columbine*: Late spring– early summer **13** *Hemerocallis*: Early–late summer
14 *Primulas*: Mid spring
15 *Lilies of the valley*: Mid–late spring **16** *Anemones*: Late summer–mid autumn

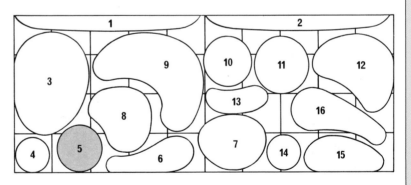

Paved Gardens

A planting scheme to add all-year-round interest and seasonal variation to an area of paving 16 foot × 14 foot. The scheme would be perfect for a small town garden or a patio.

Ingredients for a paved garden 16 foot × 14 foot

Early spring

To plant in the paving

1 *Berberis thunbergii* 'Rose Glow'

2 *Alchemilla mollis*

2 *Bergenia cordifolia*

6 *Dianthus* 'Doris'

1 *Geranium* 'Johnson's Blue'

6 *Nigella damascena*

1 *Santolina chamaecyparissus*

3 *Armeria maritima* (thrift)

12 *Mixed Godetia*

2 *Saxifraga × umbrosa* (saxifrage)

To plant in pots

1 *Camellia × Williamsii* 'Donation'

1 *Azalea mollis*

Mid spring

To plant in the paving

1 *Euonymus fortunei* 'Emerald 'n' Gold'

1 *Elaeagnus pungens* 'Maculata'

To plant in pots

3 *Agapanthus* 'Headbourne Hybrid'

Late spring

To plant in pots

5 *Begonia × semperflorens-cultorum*

10 *Petunia multiflora* 'Resisto Mixed'

1 *Pelargonium* 'Apple Blossom Orbit'

6 *Lobelia* (trailing)

5 *Impatiens* 'Pastel Mixed'

Early autumn

To plant in the paving

4 *Myosotis alpestris* 'Blue Ball' (forget-me-not)

From the garden shed

Slug traps and bait

1 bag of potting soil

1 bag of potting soil suitable for acid-loving plants

2 × 15 inch diameter pots or tubs
2 × 12 inch diameter pots
4 × 8 inch diameter pots
  all frost resistant, and with drainage holes

Bottle of liquid house-plant feed or all-purpose fertilizer

11–22 × 2 gallon bucketfuls of peat moss, garden compost or well-rotted manure

4–5 pounds 5–10–5 or other all-purpose fertilizer

Tools required

Spade

Garden fork

Rake

Hand trowel

Watering can or hose

Pruning shears

BERBERIS (medium)

ALCHEMILLA (short)

EUONYMUS
(medium)

NIGELLA (short)

GODETIA (short)

AZALEA (medium)

DIANTHUS (short)

GERANIUM (short)

ARMERIA (dwarf)

SAXIFRAGA (short)

CAMELLIA (tall)

BERGENIA (short)

PETUNIA (dwarf)

SANTOLINA (short)

BEGONIA (dwarf)

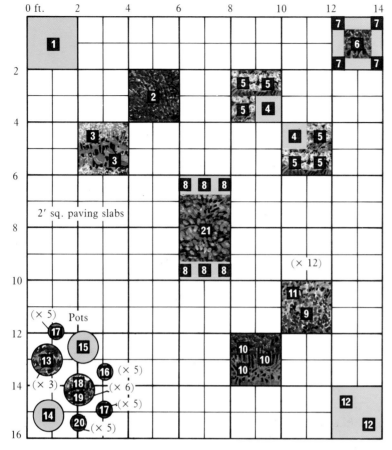

Right Paved garden. **Left** Paved garden plan. Colored areas indicate flowers in bloom in mid summer. Average flowering periods are listed below: **1** *Euonymus* **2** *Berberis*: Early–late summer **3** *Alchemilla*: Early–late summer **4** *Bergenia*: Mid–late spring **5** *Dianthus*: Early–mid summer **6** *Geranium*: Early summer–early autumn **7** *Myosotis*: Mid spring–early summer **8** *Nigella*: Early–late summer **9** *Santolina*: Mid summer **10** *Armeria*: Late spring–mid summer **11** *Godetia*: Early–late summer **12** *Saxifrage*: Mid–late spring **13** *Agapanthus*: Early–late summer **14** *Camellia*: Late autumn and winter (in the South) **15** *Azalea*: Mid–late spring **16** *Begonias*: Early summer–early autumn **17** *Petunias*: Early–late summer **18** *Pelargonium*: Early–late summer **19** *Lobelia*: Early summer–early autumn **20** *Impatiens*: Early summer–early autumn **21** *Elaeagnus*

On plan: 2′ sq. paving slabs; Pots; (× 12); (× 5); (× 3); (× 6); (× 5); (× 5)

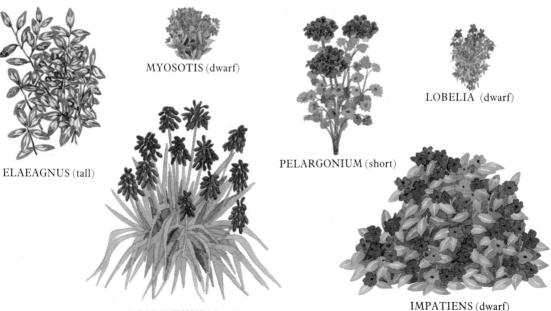

MYOSOTIS (dwarf)

LOBELIA (dwarf)

ELAEAGNUS (tall)

PELARGONIUM (short)

AGAPANTHUS (short)

IMPATIENS (dwarf)

Method

If you are starting with an existing paved area, lift and take away paving slabs approximately equivalent to those shown as removed on the plan. If you are laying a new area of paving, simply leave out the appropriate slabs to allow the necessary spaces for planting.

Good soil preparation is very important when planting in spaces between paving slabs. This is because paving is usually laid on to areas of poor soil or fill (builders' rubble), which does not provide much nourishment for plants. Unfortunately, in the limited space between paving slabs "normal" soil preparation is not so easy to do. So forget the usual method and instead dig out $\frac{1}{4}$ bucket of soil from each square foot of bed space, remove it entirely, and replace it with peat moss, compost or manure. Use a garden fork to mix the compost roughly in with the remaining soil. If the soil underneath your paving turns out to consist of a great deal of rubble with very little soil, then increase the amount you remove to $\frac{1}{2}$ bucket from each square foot, and replace with the same amount of compost.

Sprinkle 1 cup of fertilizer evenly over each square foot of the beds that have now been formed among the paving slabs, and mix it in with a garden fork.

Early spring

Planting   Plant out the berberis, alchemilla, bergenia, dianthus, geranium, santolina, armeria and saxifrage in the beds.

Place the plants, still in their pots, in the positions they are to be planted in.

Knock each in turn out of its pot, without breaking up the ball of roots inside – tap the base of the pot with the trowel handle to loosen it. Then dig a hole in the planting position the same size as the plant pot. Sit the plant in the hole, and turn its 'best' side to face the direction the plant will most often be seen from. Firm the soil very lightly down around the rootball with the handle of the trowel.

Water the plants with a hose or watering can. Give the berberis and santolina 1 gallon of water each, and the alchemilla, bergenia, dianthus, geranium, armeria and saxifrage about 1 quart each.

If slugs are a problem in your garden, set out slug traps among the plants.

To plant the azalea and, in areas north of Virginia, the camellia, first place the containers in position. Half fill each of the two largest with the special potting soil for acid-loving plants.

Stand the azalea in one and the camellia in the other, still in their pots. The rim of each pot should stand about 1 inch below the top of each container.

Knock the plants carefully out of their pots, without breaking up the ball of root, and stand each one in the center of its pot. Fill in around the roots with more of the potting soil, and firm gently down. Water the containers thoroughly, giving each one approximately 3 pints of water.

To sow the nigella and godetia, rake the soil into a fine tilth. Scatter the seeds over the surface, then rake them lightly until they are thinly covered with soil.

MAINTENANCE

In subsequent years, feed the azalea and camellia, giving each one about 3 ounces of 5–10–5 or other all-purpose fertilizer.

Special note

When the roots of a plant have penetrated down into the soil, looking at the condition of the surface is no longer enough. You need to know how moist the soil is further down, so stick your finger or the probe of an electronic water meter in to a depth of 3–4 inches. If you are still unsure whether to water or not, dig out a handful of soil and inspect it.

Mid spring

Plant the euonymus and elaeagnus in the beds, following the instructions for berberis etc.

Plant the 3 agapanthus in a group in one of the 12 inch containers, using the ordinary potting soil. Water thoroughly, giving the container about 3 pints of water.

Feed the agapanthus monthly with liquid fertilizer.

If slugs seem plentiful, set out slug traps, especially around the bergenia.

Thin the nigella and godetia seedlings to leave 6 and 12 strong plants respectively, well spaced apart.

Late spring

Plant the begonia, petunia, pelargonium, lobelia and impatiens. Fill the remaining five containers to within 1 inch of the rim with ordinary potting soil, and make small holes with the trowel just big enough to take the roots of the plants. Firm the soil gently around them, and water after planting.

Continue to feed the agapanthus.

Early summer

Watch out for the very occasional weed that may appear in the beds or containers and pull it out before it gets too big. It is still a lot less weeding than you would need to do in a "normal" garden. Feed the agapanthus.

Mid summer

When the first flush of flowers on the petunia, begonia, pelargonium, lobelia, impatiens and nigella are over, remove the dead heads with pruning shears or else nip them off between thumb and forefinger. This keeps the plants looking good, and encourages them to produce lots more flowers. Continue watching out for weeds, and give the agapanthus its monthly feed.

Late summer

Continue weeding, if necessary, and feed the agapanthus.

Early autumn

Plant the forget-me-nots following the instructions for berberis etc.

Pull out and throw away the petunia, begonia, lobelia, impatiens, godetia and nigella after flowering.

Keep the pelargonium if you have a warm greenhouse or a windowsill indoors where it can live for the winter. Dig it out of its container and place in a small plastic pot with a little potting soil around the roots.

Tip out the soil from the empty containers and clean them thoroughly with hot water and a stiff brush.

If you have space in a shed or garage to store them they can be put right away until next spring.

When the geranium, forget-me-nots, bergenia and alchemilla start to die back naturally, cut their leaves back to ground level and remove any debris.

The dianthus, armeria and saxifrage may need a little light pruning to keep them looking neat – select straggly or broken shoots and use pruning shears to cut the entire shoot right back to its base.

> **In subsequent years**, the elaeagnus, santolina, berberis and euonymus may require light pruning to keep them in shape or repair physical damage; cut out entire shoots back to a main branch to make them look neat. This way you also avoid leaving untidy "snags" where plant diseases start up.

Mid autumn

Plant the camellia, in areas south of Virginia, following the instructions on page 70 for camellias.

Reduce the water you give to the plants and stop feeding them. In southern climates azaleas and camellias need another feed now; give them 3 ounces of 5–10–5 or other all-purpose fertilizer.

Late autumn

Prepare the plants in containers for winter.

Keep the agapanthus in its container and stand it in a frost-free shed, greenhouse or porch for the winter. The camellia may be left outside, provided your paved garden is reasonably well sheltered from wind and in a part of the country that is not liable to very severe winters. North of Maryland, it is advisable to move it, still in its container, inside a frost-free greenhouse or porch for the winter. It must be kept in the light so a dark shed is unacceptable except as a very temporary measure.

In exceptionally cold climates, the azalea may need to be kept in a greenhouse for winter, but in most places it is sufficient to insulate the pot with newspaper, plastic or burlap to protect the roots from very hard freezing. Do not leave the container standing in a puddle of water; if necessary raise it up on some bricks to ensure that excess water can drain away from the plant.

Purely Perennial

This low-maintenance scheme uses perennials. Buy the following plants instead of those shown in brackets.

Early spring

To plant in the paving

2 *Hosta fortunei* 'Albopicta' (replace *Berberis thunbergii* 'Rose Glow')

1 *Gypsophila paniculata* 'Bristol Fairy' (replaces *Elaeagnus pungens* 'Maculata')

2 *Campanula lactiflora* (replace *Nigella damascena*)

To plant in pots

1 *Nepeta* × *faassenii* (replaces *Petunia* in first pot)

1 *Helianthemum nummularium* (replaces *Impatiens*)

Mid spring

To plant in the paving

4 *Anaphalis triplinervis* (replace *Santolina chamaecyparissus* and *Godetia*)

To plant in pots

1 *Sedum spectabile* 'Autumn Joy' (replaces *Azalea mollis*)

1 *Campanula carpatica* 'Jingle Bells' (replaces *Petunia* in second pot)

3 *Sempervivum* 'Species Mixed' (replace *Begonia* × *semperflorens-cultorum*)

1 *Yucca filamentosa* (replaces *Pelargonium* 'Apple Blossom Orbit' and *Lobelia*)

Tools required

Hedging shears

SEDUM (short)

HOSTA (short)

CAMPANULA LACTIFLORA (medium)

YUCCA (short)

SEMPERVIVUM (dwarf)

GYPSOPHILA (medium)

CAMPANULA CARPATICA (dwarf)

HELIANTHEMUM (dwarf)

ANAPHALIS (short)

Early spring Plant out the hosta, *Campanula lactiflora* and gypsophila, following the planting and watering instructions for the berberis etc on page 70.

Plant the nepeta and helianthemum in pots, following the potting, feeding and watering instructions for begonia etc on page 71.

Mid spring Plant the anaphalis, following the planting and watering instructions for the berberis etc on page 70.

Plant the sedum, *Campanula carpatica*, sempervivums and yucca, following the potting, feeding and watering instructions for begonia etc on page 71.

11										**20**
										14

1

13 (× 3)
19 (× 1)

12

19 (× 1)
13 (× 3)

2

2′ sq paving slabs

3

4

Pots

6
5
18
8
9
7
17
10
15
16

1 *Hostas:* Mid summer **2** *Gypsophila:* Early summer–late summer **3** *Campanula lactiflora:* Early summer–mid summer **4** *Anaphalis:* Late summer **5** *Sedum:* Late summer–early autumn **6** *Nepeta:* Late spring–late summer **7** *Campanula carpatica:* Early summer–mid summer **8** *Sempervivums* **9** *Yucca* **10** *Helianthemum:* Mid summer **11** *Euonymus* **12** *Alchemilla* **13** *Dianthus* **14** *Myosotis* **15** *Armeria* **16** *Saxifrage* **17** *Camellia* **18** *Agapanthus* **19** *Bergenia* **20** *Geranium*

Mid summer Cut back the helianthemum with shears after flowering to encourage further flowering.

Late summer Remove flower stems of *Campanula lactiflora*, after flowering.

Early autumn If the anaphalis has become untidy, cut it back hard. Cut back the nepeta. Leave the dead stems on the sedum until spring.

Protect the yucca and helianthemum from being damaged by strong winds: move the pots to a more sheltered place and insulate all pots as described on page 72 in severe weather. In the case of the yucca and helianthemum, tie the leaves together with fabric strips. Uncover the plants when weather permits.

Check that the pots are not standing in water.

Late autumn When the foliage of sedum and *Campanula carpatica* starts to die back naturally, cut them down level with the top of the pots. Cut flower stems and leaves of hostas and gypsophila to ground level.

NEPETA (short)

Mainly Evergreen

In this variation mainly evergreen plants provide a permanent backdrop of blue, gold, green and red foliage against which seasonal highlights are picked out with colorful annuals. Again, it requires only very little maintenance.

You will not have to buy berberis, bergenia, dianthus, geranium, forget-me-nots, armeria, godetia or saxifrage and will need only 3 nigella instead of 6. All the plants in pots remain as in the main plan.

Early spring

1 *Gypsophila paniculata* 'Bristol Fairy'

Mid spring

1 *Chamaecyparis pisifera* 'Boulevard'

1 *Lonicera japonica* 'Halliana' (honeysuckle)

3 *Juniperus squamata* 'Meyeri'

1 *Phormium tenax* 'Purpureum'

1 *Juniperus horizontalis*

1 *Chamaecyparis pisifera* 'Filifera Aurea'

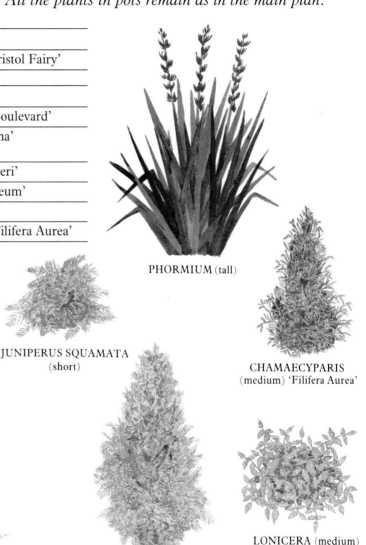

PHORMIUM (tall)

JUNIPERUS SQUAMATA (short)

CHAMAECYPARIS (medium) 'Filifera Aurea'

GYPSOPHILA (medium)

LONICERA (medium)

JUNIPERUS HORIZONTALIS (dwarf)

CHAMAECYPARIS (tall) 'Boulevard'

Early spring   Plant the gypsophila following the instructions for berberis etc on page 70.

Mid spring   Plant the chamaecyparis, honeysuckle, juniper and phormium following the instructions for berberis etc on page 70.

> Replacement and additional plants are given at the start of each variation. For quantities of original plants, uncolored in the planting plan and not given in the variation ingredients, check with the list at the start of the main plan.

> **In subsequent years**, mulch the honeysuckle with leaf mold or well-rotted compost. If the junipers or chamaecyparis have broken or awkwardly shaped branches cut them back to a main branch or the stem using pruning shears. Avoid snipping off odd bits as this can leave the plant open to disease.

Mid summer   Pay particular attention to watering as newly planted evergreens, particularly conifers, are very susceptible to browning foliage if they are allowed to get too dry. Remember that plants growing in paving will not be able to benefit from rainfall as much as those growing in a border.

Late summer   Remove dead flower stems from the phormium.

Mid autumn   Cut down the gypsophila. Prune the honeysuckle, removing whole branches rather than a lot of twigs.

Early winter   Protect the phormium from frost with straw or bracken.

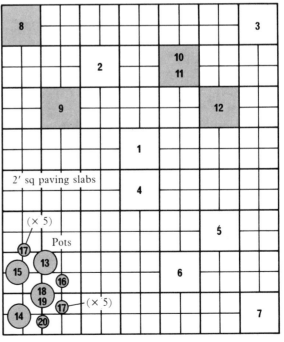

1 *Gypsophila:* Early summer–late summer
2 *Chamaecyparis* ('Boulevard')
3 *Honeysuckle:* Mid spring–late spring
4 *Juniperus squamata*   5 *Phormium*
6 *Juniperus horizontalis*
7 *Chaemacyparis* ('Filifera Aurea')
8 *Elaeagnus*   9 *Alchemilla*
10 *Santolina*   11 *Nigella*   12 *Euonymus*
13 *Azalea*   14 *Camellia*   15 *Agapanthus*
16 *Begonia*   17 *Petunias*   18 *Pelargonium*
19 *Lobelia*   20 *Impatiens*

Introducing Bulbs

This variation, the only one in the book which requires only autumn planting, introduces spring color. The ingredients are the same as for the main plan, with the following bulbs:

Early autumn

To plant in the paving

12 *Scilla sibirica*

24 *Galanthus nivalis* (snowdrops)

12 *Chionodoxa luciliae*

12 *Narcissus* 'Cheerfulness'

24 *Anemone blanda* (mixed colours)

12 *Muscari armeniacum*

12 *Galtonia candicans*

To plant in pots

6 *Narcissus* Jonquil type

6 *Iris unguicularis*

6 *Iris reticulata*

6 *Narcissus triandrus albus*

6 *Narcissus* 'Cheerfulness'

Mid autumn

To plant in the paving

24 *Tulipa fosteriana* 'Red Emperor'

From the garden shed

2 × 2 gallon bucketfuls of peat, well-rotted compost or manure (for poor soil only)

1 bag of potting soil

NARCISSUS
'Cheerfulness'
(short)

NARCISSUS
'Jonquil'
(short)

NARCISSUS
'Albus'
(short)

TULIPA
(short)

IRIS RETICULATA
(dwarf)

ANEMONE (dwarf)

GALANTHUS
(dwarf)

IRIS UNGUICULARIS
(dwarf)

MUSCARI (dwarf)

CHIONODOXA (dwarf)

SCILLA (dwarf)

Early autumn Plant the narcissus 'Cheerfulness', scilla, snowdrops, chionodoxa, anemone and muscari in the beds which contain berberis etc (see plan). Group them in natural-looking clumps among the plants.

Move to the remaining beds and space the bulbs all over the area to create a "carpet" of color.

Use a small trowel and scoop out a hole 4 inches deep for small bulbs such as snowdrops, scilla and muscari, and 6 inches deep for larger bulbs like narcissi. (Note that this is slightly deeper than is sometimes recommended, since these bulbs will be in place permanently.)

Press each bulb down firmly into the bottom of the hole, pointed end up, with a slight screwing motion. This makes sure the base of the bulb is in firm contact with the soil, which will help it root in. If the soil is very poor, dig a hole 2 inches deeper before planting and place a handful of peat moss or well-rotted compost under each bulb.

Now replace the soil around and over the bulb, and continue until all are planted. There is no need to water bulbs in after planting.

To plant bulbs in the pots, half fill with fresh potting soil. Plant the iris and narcissi bulbs, one variety per container, saving the larger narcissus 'Cheerfulness' for the biggest container. Press each bulb in turn firmly down into the soil, and then fill the container to within 1 inch of the rim with more soil. Water in very lightly – just enough to moisten the soil thoroughly. Provided you have bought large bulbs, they should all flower the following spring.

Mid autumn Plant the tulip bulbs 6 inches deep following the instructions for scilla etc.

Grid plan labels: 11, 1, 4 (× 12), 7 (× 6), 16, 17, 10, 12, 15 (× 3), 14 (× 1), 2, (× 12), 13, 14 (× 1), 15 (× 3), 2, (× 12), 26, 4 (× 12), 7 (× 6), 2' sq paving slabs, 18, 5, (× 12), Pots, 19, 21, 6, 8, 25, 23, 9, 20, 5, (× 6), 8, 24, 9, 3, 22

1	Scilla	2	Galanthus	3	Chionodoxa	4	Tulips
5	Narcissus ('Cheerfulness')	6	Anemones				
7	Muscari	8	Narcissus	9	Iris		
10	Galtonia	11	Euonymus	12	Berberis		
13	Alchemilla	14	Bergenia	15	Dianthus		
16	Geranium	17	Myosotis	18	Nigella	19	Santolina
20	Armeria	21	Godetia	22	Saxifrage	23	Agapanthus
24	Camellia	25	Azalea	26	Elaeagnus		

The following spring, after flowering, nip the dead heads off but do not cut the foliage back or tie it in knots, as is often done. Instead let it die back naturally, and when it is completely yellow or brown cut it off at ground level and clear it away. Bulbs growing in containers may be dug out and replanted elsewhere after flowering – there is no need to wait until the foliage dies back if you do it carefully and avoid damaging the roots. Mark the spot where you plant them, and you can dig the same bulbs up again next autumn to replant in the original containers. In the meantime, the same set of containers can be used for summer bedding plants.

With Herbs

This variation introduces a cottage flavor – not to mention scent – to the basic theme, using a mixture of decorative and ornamental herbs. Buy the following plants instead of those shown in brackets.

Early spring

To plant in the paving

2 *Lavandula spica* 'Hidcote' (lavender) (replace *Bergenia cordifolia*

1 *Rosmarinus officinalis* (rosemary) (replaces *Geranium* 'Johnson's Blue')

1 *Angelica archangelica* (angelica) (replaces *Saxifraga* × *umbrosa*)

Late spring

To plant in the paving

2 *Salvia officinalis* (sage) (replace *Elaeagnus pungens* 'Maculata')

4 *Origanum vulgare* 'Aureum' (golden oregano), and
2 *Allium schoenoprasum* (chives) (replace *Armeria maritima*)

To plant in pots

5 *Anethum graveolens* (dill) (replace *Azalea mollis*)

5 *Petroselinum crispum* (parsley) (replace *Pelargonium* 'Apple Blossom Orbit' and *Lobelia*)

From the garden shed

1 bag all-purpose potting soil

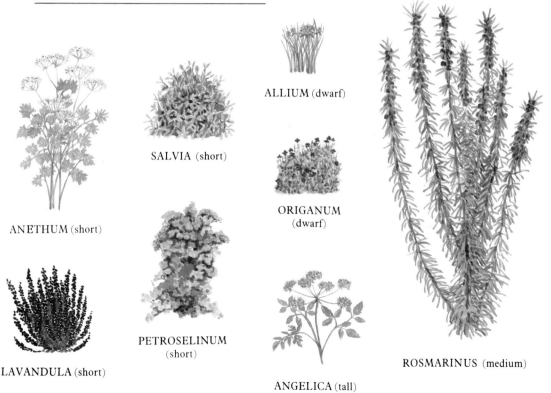

ALLIUM (dwarf)

SALVIA (short)

ORIGANUM
(dwarf)

ANETHUM (short)

PETROSELINUM
(short)

LAVANDULA (short)

ANGELICA (tall)

ROSMARINUS (medium)

Early spring   Plant out the lavender, rosemary and angelica, following the instructions for berberis etc on page 70.

Late spring   Plant out the dill, parsley, oregano, sage and chives following the instructions for begonia etc on page 71.

In subsequent years, replant dill and parsley.

Early to mid autumn   Pull out the parsley and dill and throw them away. Cut down the chives and marjoram as they die back for winter.

Prune the rosemary and sage slightly, to help them retain their shape. Use sharp pruning shears, and simply cut out any broken or untidy branches right back to a main branch. Cut back the lavender lightly, with shears.

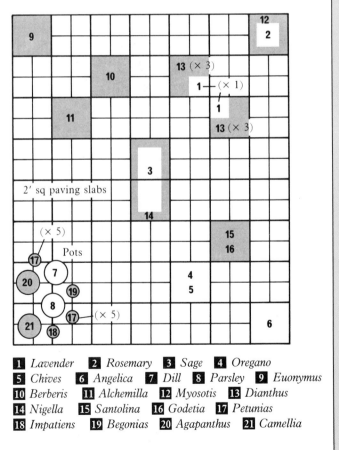

1 *Lavender*   2 *Rosemary*   3 *Sage*   4 *Oregano*
5 *Chives*   6 *Angelica*   7 *Dill*   8 *Parsley*   9 *Euonymus*
10 *Berberis*   11 *Alchemilla*   12 *Myosotis*   13 *Dianthus*
14 *Nigella*   15 *Santolina*   16 *Godetia*   17 *Petunias*
18 *Impatiens*   19 *Begonias*   20 *Agapanthus*   21 *Camellia*

Rose Gardens

The main plan is for a formal rose garden and subtle variations to the basic scheme introduce new ideas to this theme. Depending on where you live, early spring or late winter is the best time to plant a new rose garden. Roses can be planted in autumn in mild climates or with good winter protection; or any time during the spring and summer provided you only use container-grown roses. Never try to transplant roses dug up from another bed between mid spring and early autumn when the plants are growing. Roses are mostly planted in early spring; in the South and Southwest and in southern California, they are planted in winter.

Ingredients for a rose bed 10 foot × 5 foot

Early spring

3 Floribunda 'Allgold'

3 Grandiflora 'Pink Parfait'

2 Hybrid tea 'Chicago Peace'

2 Miniature 'Baby Masquerade'

2 Miniature 'Baby Darling'

From the garden shed

Rose fungicide

Plant pesticide

Small hand sprayer

Packet commercial rose food, or 10–10–10 or 5–10–10 fertilizer

Small amount of 0–10–10 fertilizer for last feeding in autumn

11 × 2 gallon bucketfuls well-rotted horse manure for top dressing

Tools required

Spade

Garden fork

Rake

Garden line

Hand trowel

Watering can or hose

Pruning shears

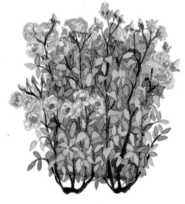

FLORIBUNDA
(medium) 'Allgold'

MINIATURE
(dwarf)
'Baby Darling'

HYBRID TEA
(tall)

MINIATURE
(dwarf)
'Baby Masquerade'

GRANDIFLORA
(medium)

Method

Choose a sunny situation and mark out an area 10 foot × 5 foot with a garden line or four stakes and a ball of string. The bed is best cut into a lawn. To keep the formality of the scheme, be sure to line it up so that it runs parallel with any straight feature already in the garden, such as the boundary fence or wall, a path or the edge of a patio. Prepare the soil as described in the introduction.

Early spring

'Bare root' roses (i.e. roses which have not been grown in containers but have been dug up from a bed and sold with their roots wrapped in plastic or other material) are planted now.

Before planting Soak the roots in a bucket of tepid water for an hour. After taking the plants out, use pruning shears to carefully trim away any dead or broken bits of root to avoid infections starting in them. At the same time, shorten any roots that are noticeably longer than the others. This makes it easier to plant them properly, and does not harm them in the least.

Now prune the top of the plants, if the nurseryman has not already done this. Cut all of the stems of the hybrid tea roses back to within 4 inches of the point where they originate from the main stem, and those of the floribundas and grandifloras to 6 inches. Prune the miniature roses back to remove about half their height. In each case, cut just above a leaf joint, though it can sometimes be a little difficult to tell exactly where they are if the stems have lost their leaves.

MAINTENANCE

In subsequent years, prune the roses, using sharp pruning shears and cutting any dead or thin, weak shoots out entirely, right back to the base. Then cut all the stems of the hybrid tea roses down to about 6 inches above ground level, and all the stems of the floribundas and grandifloras down to 8 inches. Miniature roses need hardly any pruning – just cut them back by about half their height. In all cases, cut neatly just above a leaf as it is from this point that the new shoots will grow.

Feed after pruning, using rose fertilizer or 10–10–10 or 5–10–10 at the rate recommended by the manufacturer. Next give the soil a light cultivation to aerate it. You can use the points of a garden fork to loosen the soil, but do not actually dig it or you may damage the roots of the plants. Alternatively, hoe thoroughly. Spread a mulch of well-rotted horse manure over the bed.

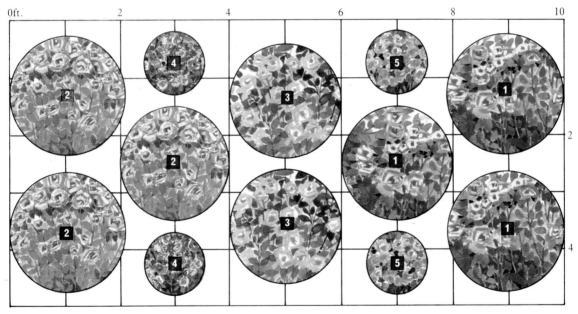

Top Rose garden. **Above** Rose garden plan. Colored areas indicate roses in bloom in midsummer. Average flowering periods are listed below:

1 *Grandiflora* 'Pink Parfait': Early summer–mid summer, early autumn–mid autumn **2** *Floribunda* 'Allgold': Early summer–late summer
3 *Hybrid tea* 'Chicago Peace': Early summer–mid autumn **4** *Miniature* 'Baby Masquerade': Early summer–mid summer **5** *Miniature* 'Baby Darling': Early summer–mid summer

(Early spring)

Planting To plant 'bare root' roses, dig a hole rather bigger than the maximum root spread of your rose. Look for the mark on the stem which shows the previous soil level and aim to plant to the same depth again.

Fork over the bottom of the hole to loosen the soil. Stand the plant in the hole and spread the roots out over the bottom of it so they are as far apart as possible. Now place a couple of trowelfuls of soil over the roots to anchor them in place. Very gently firm the soil down with your foot. Fill in the rest of the hole with soil.

Now check to see that the soil mark on the stem matches up with the new level of soil around it. If the plant is too far out of the ground, dig it up and start again. If it is slightly too deep, hold it by the main stem and gently jiggle it about in the soil until you raise it up to the correct level. When the level is correct, firm the soil lightly down all around the plant with your foot.

If you are planting container-grown roses in spring, prune as described for bare root roses. Then simply knock the plant out of its container (give the bottom a sharp tap with the handle of the trowel to loosen it first). The container should fit snugly into the hole, its rim level with the soil surface. Remove it and fork over the bottom of the hole to loosen the soil.

Just before planting, check the condition of the rootball. If the base is just a tight mass of thickly coiled roots, gently tease a few of these out. Then stand the plant in the hole and fill in around the roots with soil. Firm the soil down gently around the rootball with your foot.

It is best to wait a year before cutting roses for the house. The bushes will be well established and producing more flowers than they did in the first year. Avoid taking too many flowers from any one bush at a time and just cut one or two from each instead.

When cutting roses, always take a bucketful of fresh water with you. Use sharp pruning shears and cut the stems off cleanly just above a leaf, as if you were pruning. Strip the leaves and thorns from the lower third to half of each cut stem and stand them straight in the bucket of water.

When you have cut enough, take the flowers indoors and keep them in a cool place for an hour before you arrange them. Try to cut the stems to the right length under water and put them into a vase filled with fresh water to which a cut flower preservative has been added. This will ensure they last as long as possible.

(Early spring)

Water in the roses, giving each plant about ½ gallon of water. If the soil is very dry give the entire bed a thorough soaking, using the hose with your finger partly covering the end of it to produce a fine spray.

Follow up by top dressing the ground between the plants with a layer of well-rotted horse manure.

> To plant container-grown roses during summer follow instructions for planting container-grown roses in spring, but do not prune.

Mid to late spring

Check newly planted roses regularly every week to see if they need watering. Dig out a handful of soil to the full depth of the trowel to see if it looks or feels dry. If it does, then water thoroughly.

A traditional rose garden like this which has bare soil between the plants needs weeding every week. Any weeds, even small ones, will quickly spoil the appearance of the bed. A hoe is the easiest way of keeping on top of the fast-growing annual weeds which appear quickly in wet weather.

Throughout summer

Water new roses whenever the soil becomes very dry.

Feed regularly, using a commercial rose fertilizer or 10–10–10 or 5–10–10, and following the manufacturer's instructions.

Deadhead the flowers as soon as the first flush is over and make it a weekly routine from then on as this will encourage more flowers to bloom. When deadheading, use pruning shears and cut off the old flower heads a short way down the stem, just above a healthy green leaf.

Examine the plants every week or two to see if they have become infested with aphids, generally found in colonies towards the top of the plant on young shoots, flower buds and the undersides of young leaves. Twisted and contorted leaves are one unpleasant side-effect they produce; another is a nasty black sticky goo that eventually covers the plants. Unfortunately this can only be removed by wiping each leaf individually, front and back, and unless the aphids causing it are killed it will soon return. A few aphids are unlikely to do very much harm, but if numbers increase then you should certainly get rid of them.

(Throughout summer)

Special note

When mixing pesticides use a small hand sprayer and mix the pesticide in it to avoid getting any on your hands. Spray in the early morning or evening, when the sun is not shining on to the plants. Also avoid windy weather. Spray each plant until the spray starts to drip off the leaves. Try to cover each leaf on both sides and get the spray well down into the center of each plant. Dispose of any left-over spray. Place it in a sealed container; do not pour it down the sink or a drain.

Spray every two weeks with any good general plant pesticide following the manufacturer's instructions.

It is also advisable to spray regularly against blackspot. Affected plants produce characteristic black marks on their leaves. To keep your plants free of these you will need to spray with a special rose fungicide every two weeks (or as directed by the manufacturers).

Watch out for weeds, which will be starting to grow on top of the manure layer.

Remove any suckers from the roses as soon as they appear. These are very strong, fast-growing shoots that appear from below ground level around the plant and they will rapidly overrun the rose, unless you remove them. Do not cut them off with pruning shears, as this just makes them worse. Take a fork and dig down near the rose until you find where the sucker grows out from a root. Then tear it out, so you remove a tiny "heel" of the root with it. In this way it will not be able to grow back again. Fill in the hole and replace the top dressing of manure over the area.

Early autumn

Check for the first signs of mildew. This appears as a powdery substance over some of the leaves, stems and flower buds; as it gets worse it may cover large areas of the plant and some of the leaves may even be shed. Mildew can be especially troublesome in cool, humid weather. Spray with the general rose fungicide that you used during the summer to prevent blackspot. Repeat every two weeks until the end of the autumn.

Mid autumn

Give the roses a small final feed with 0–10–10. Prune lightly in mild areas, and prune and prepare for winter protection elsewhere. All that is necessary for pruning is to shorten their stems by about half to prevent windrock. Do not bother about cutting neatly just above a leaf-joint as is normally done – a rough cut about halfway up each stem is all that is needed for floribundas, grandifloras and hybrid tea roses. Do not prune the miniatures. Remove the prunings, weed and leave the bed tidy ready for winter.

For winter protection, tie the pruned stems together with twine and mound soil 8 inches deep around the base of each plant. When the soil mound freezes later in autumn, place a hardware cloth or chicken wire cylinder around each plant and fill it with 8–10 inches of leaves or other loose mulch atop the soil mound. Leave the mulch and soil mound in place until after your last hard frost the following spring.

With Ground Cover Plants

In the original plan, the roses are surrounded by bare soil; in this variation evergreen ground cover plants provide a permanent background to the flowers and also supply interest of their own outside the normal rose season. Once established, they cut down on a lot of the routine weeding, too! They will cover the ground entirely and weeds will not be able to grow through the carpet of foliage covering the bed. If a perennial weed occasionally manages to push through, pull it carefully. For this variation you do not need the Miniature roses 'Baby Masquerade' and 'Baby Darling'.

Early to mid spring

16 *Lamium maculatum* 'Beacon Silver'

12 *Iberis sempervirens* (perennial candytuft)

From the garden shed

About 30 × 8 inch lengths of flexible wire

LAMIUM (dwarf)

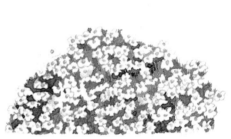

IBERIS (dwarf)

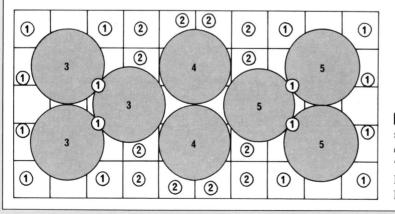

1 *Lamium*: Early summer–mid summer   **2** *Iberis*: Late spring–early summer   **3** *Floribunda* 'Allgold'   **4** *Hybrid tea* 'Chicago Peace'   **5** *Grandiflora* 'Pink Parfait'

Early to mid spring Plant the lamium and iberis. Knock them out of their containers by giving the base a sharp tap with the handle of the trowel. Dig the holes exactly the same size as the containers, and fork over the bottom of each hole. Tease a few of the roots free of the rootball and stand the plants in the holes. Fill round the roots with soil, and firm down with your foot.

Mid to late spring Begin to peg the runners of lamium down to the soil, encouraging them to run in all directions. Hold the runners down with wire pegs made by bending 8 inch lengths of wire in half to make "hairpins", and pushing them into the ground either side of a shoot. The pieces pegged down will root and become new plants.

Early summer Continue pegging down lamium shoots.

Feed the entire bed with rose fertilizer (see page 86), washing the granules off the leaves of the lamium and iberis with a hose afterwards.

Remove the developing flower spikes from the lamium.

Weed or hoe carefully between the plants. Alternatively, you can use a weedkiller intended for flowers – those intended for use among shrubs are not usually suitable to use with ground cover plants. Be careful not to exceed the stated dose or it may inhibit the growth of the plants.

Mid summer Snip off the dead flower heads from the iberis.

Continue pegging down the lamium shoots, and feeding the bed with fertilizer. Continue weeding or hoeing.

Late summer Continue weeding, as above.

Mid autumn Stand on the grass round the bed to prune the roses. Avoid walking on the soil.

Replacement and additional plants are given at the start of each variation. For quantities of original plants, uncolored in the planting plan and not given in the variation ingredients, check with the list at the start of the main plan.

In subsequent years, in **spring**, hoe where possible between the lamium and iberis to loosen the soil, but take care not to chop through their stems. As far as you are able, top dress between the plants with a mulch of well-rotted horse manure.

With Dwarf Shrubs

This variation creates an informal border where roses are teamed with dwarf shrubs for a charming cottagey effect. You do not need Floribunda 'Allgold', Grandiflora 'Pink Parfait' or Miniature 'Baby Masquerade'.

Early spring

1 Miniature 'Baby Darling' (replaces 2)

2 Prostrate rose 'Nozomi'

From the garden shed

About 2½ yards flexible wire to cut into 8 inch lengths

Mid spring

2 *Salvia officinalis* 'Purpurea'

3 *Santolina chamaecyparissus*

3 *Lavandula spica* 'Hidcote' (lavender)

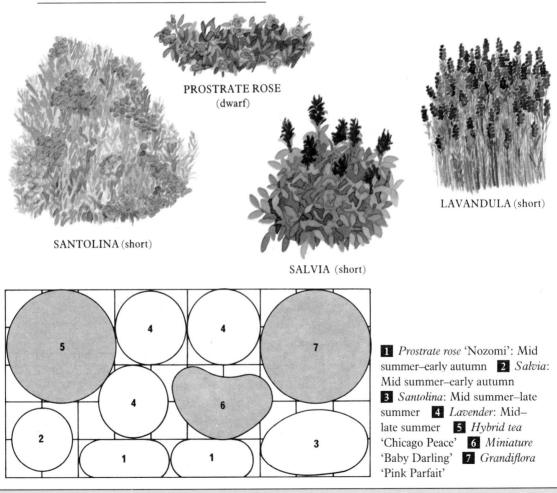

PROSTRATE ROSE (dwarf)

LAVANDULA (short)

SANTOLINA (short)

SALVIA (short)

1 *Prostrate rose* 'Nozomi': Mid summer–early autumn **2** *Salvia*: Mid summer–early autumn **3** *Santolina*: Mid summer–late summer **4** *Lavender*: Mid–late summer **5** *Hybrid tea* 'Chicago Peace' **6** *Miniature* 'Baby Darling' **7** *Grandiflora* 'Pink Parfait'

Early spring　Plant the prostrate rose Nozomi following the method described on page 85, but do not prune it.

Mid spring　Plant the salvia, santolina and lavender. Knock them out of their pots by giving the base a sharp tap with the handle of the trowel. Dig holes the same size as the containers and loosen the soil at the bottom of the hole with a fork. Tease the roots out a little from the rootballs and place the plants into the holes, firming the soil down gently.

Special note
The main purpose of pruning is to maintain a good shape and to remove any weak or dead shoots. To check whether a shoot is dead or not, look at the inside of it. If it is dead it will be a dull brown color, while a live, healthy shoot will be a green or creamy color inside. When you are removing dead shoots, cut back cleanly to just above a live bud so that there is no dead wood left to encourage further die-back.

In subsequent years, remove any shoots of Nozomi which have grown untidy or have died. Nozomi does not require pruning like normal roses.

Early summer　Start feeding the beds regularly. This is especially important as the shrubs will be competing for the same feed needed by the roses. Wash down the shrubs with the hose after feeding to remove any granules of fertilizer that have become lodged in the foliage. This could otherwise scorch the leaves and spoil their appearance.

Mid summer　Remove the flowers of the santolina if you prefer. They are not especially attractive, and in this scheme the plant is used for its decorative silver foliage rather than its flowers.

Remove the dead flower heads of Nozomi when deadheading the other roses (see page 86). Peg its stems down to the ground with pieces of bent wire to hold them in place. The plant should in time form a low mound, and may require slight encouragement to form a nice shape.

Late summer　Continue deadheading Nozomi with the other roses.

Early autumn　Clip the lavender and santolina with shears to remove the dead flower heads and to reshape the plants generally.

In subsequent years, clip back lavender, santolina and salvia if they become overgrown, but do not cut them hard back. Lavender especially must not be cut back to old wood (which is darker in color) as it may die rather than produce any new shoots; use shears.

Mid autumn　Prune the roses as described on page 87, except for Nozomi, which needs no pruning.

Fragrant

Fragrance is one of the main attractions of a real old-fashioned rose garden, but one in which many of the newer varieties of rose are unfortunately lacking. This variation brings together some of the most attractively perfumed varieties to create a sweetly scented rose garden.

Early spring

3 Floribunda 'English Rose' (replace floribunda 'Allgold')

3 Floribunda 'Little Darling' (replace grandiflora 'Pink Parfait')

2 Hybrid tea 'Alec's Red' (replace hybrid tea 'Chicago Peace')

4 Miniature 'Sweet Fairy' (replace miniature 'Baby Masquerade' and miniature 'Baby Darling')

MINIATURE
(dwarf)

FLORIBUNDA
'Little Darling' (medium)

FLORIBUNDA
'English Rose' (medium)

Early spring Prepare the bed and plant as on pages 83 and 85, substituting the roses listed here for those in the original plan. Their subsequent care is exactly as described on pages 86 and 87.

HYBRID TEA (medium)

1 *Floribunda* 'English Rose': Early summer–mid summer
2 *Floribunda* 'Little Darling': Early summer–mid summer
3 *Hybrid tea* 'Alec's Red': Early summer–late summer
4 *Miniature* 'Sweet Fairy': Early summer–mid summer

With Extra Height

There are many occasions when a little extra height can add variety to a rose bed. In a large garden, or where you want to situate the bed towards the back of an area, height can make all the difference. The final variation introduces standard roses to the original theme without losing its traditional formality. You will not need grandiflora 'Pink Parfait'.

Early spring

1 Extra floribunda 'Allgold'

2 Standard trained hybrid tea 'National Trust'

1 *Standard trained hybrid tea* 'National Trust': Early summer–late summer **2** *Floribunda* 'Allgold' **3** *Miniature* 'Baby Masquerade' **4** *Hybrid tea* 'Chicago Peace' **5** *Miniature* 'Baby Darling'

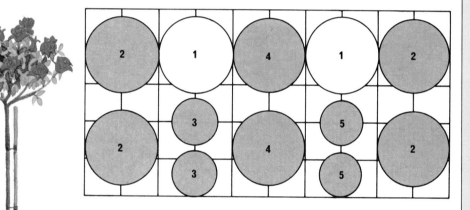

HYBRID TEA
(medium)

Early spring

Prepare the ground and plant the roses as on pages 83 and 85. Prune the standard roses by cutting the stems forming the head of the plant back to within 4 inches of the point where they originate from the trunk.

In subsequent years, prune the head of the plant, cutting each shoot back to within 6 inches of its point of origin from the trunk. As always, cut just above a leaf joint to avoid the stems dying back.

Throughout summer Remove any suckers growing from around the standard roses (see page 87) together with any shoots growing from the trunk so as to keep a clean stem.

Mid autumn Cut back the stems forming the heads of the standard roses by about half their length.

Conifer Beds

For a truly all-year-round garden, conifers can't be beaten. These striking plants offer a bit of everything – evergreen foliage, eye-catching colors, contrasting textures, a huge range of architectural shapes, even colored cones – yet require very little maintenance. The variations combine conifers in groups designed to bring out the best of their particular characteristics, while the main plan shows how to make the most of their incredible range of attractions in a small plot.

Ingredients for a bed 15 foot × 15 foot

Mid spring

3 *Chamaecyparis obtusa* 'Nana'

3 *Thuja orientalis* 'Aurea'

1 *Abies koreana*

3 *Picea glauca* 'Conica'

3 *Juniperus sabina* 'Tamariscifolia'

1 *Chamaecyparis pisifera* 'Boulevard'

From the garden shed

12 × 2 gallon bucketfuls of bark chips, straw or garden compost for mulching (optional)

Plant stakes and tree ties (see 'Maintenance', Mid spring)

1 inch nails

7 × 7 foot poles

30 foot burlap or 5 foot wide heavy plastic or anti-desiccant spray

Tools required

Spade

Garden fork

Rake

Garden line

Hand trowel

Watering can or hose and lawn sprinkler

Pruning shears

Hedging shears, hoe (optional)

THUJA ORIENTALIS
(short)

CHAMAECYPARIS PISIFERA (tall)

Method

Choose a sunny site for conifers, and preferably one that is slightly sheltered from the worst of the winter winds. Lay out the bed with a garden line. It should be cut into a lawn, as the plan is for an island bed. As it is a formal shape, the bed should be aligned to run parallel with any existing straight features in the garden, such as the side of the house, the garden fence or a path. Prepare the soil as described in the introduction.

Conifers are available in containers or, less often, with their roots in a ball of soil wrapped in sacking. Either way, buy strong, healthy plants that are a good green color all the way down to the pot, with no browning of the lower branches. Choose small plants in preference to large ones; they will become established much faster. Large conifers can be riskier to establish, and are more demanding to look after.

PICEA (medium)

ABIES (tall)

CHAMAECYPARIS OBTUSA (tall)

JUNIPERUS (short)

Mid spring

Before planting Give container-grown conifers a thorough watering and let them stand for 12 hours to soak up plenty of moisture. If you are using balled and burlapped plants, untie the wrappings and soak the roots in a bucketful of tepid water for an hour before planting. Try not to remove any soil from the roots in the process.

Stand the conifers in their positions on the prepared bed.

Planting To plant container-grown conifers, dig a hole big enough to take the container, leaving its rim level with the surrounding soil. Fork over the soil at the bottom of the hole to loosen it slightly. If the plant is in a rigid pot knock it out, first giving the bottom of the pot a sharp tap with the trowel handle to loosen it.

Check the base of the rootball; if it is a mass of tightly coiled roots, gently tease a few of these out. This will help the plant to get established and grow better, since the roots will be able to find their way out into the surrounding soil faster.

Stand the plant in the hole. Turn it so that its best side faces the outside of the bed and fill in around the roots with soil. Finally, firm the soil gently around the rootball with your foot.

To plant balled and burlapped conifers, dig a hole slightly wider than the rootball and about the same depth. It is important not to make the hole too deep; the idea is to replant at the same depth the conifer was growing at the nursery. Look for the mark on the stem which shows where the soil came to previously, and aim to have this correspond to the new soil level.

MAINTENANCE

Stake any particularly tall conifers to support them while they become established. Take a strong plant stake 18 inches longer than the height of the plant and hammer it into the ground about 4–6 inches away from the trunk, taking care not to damage the rootball.

Use strips of cloth or pieces of heavy wire slipped through sections of old rubber garden hose to secure the trunk to the stake.

Protect newly planted conifers from the wind after planting. This is very important, as otherwise they can very quickly turn brown. Once they have done so they do not generally recover unless the damage is only slight.

There are two ways to protect conifers from windy weather. The first is to put up a temporary screen of burlap or heavy plastic round the whole bed. This calls for a support structure sturdy enough to hold the wind-break steady even in fairly strong winds. Seven 7 foot poles with a point at one end hammered in 18 inches deep around the windward side of the bed, at 5 foot intervals, will suffice. Nail the burlap or plastic to them, stretching it tightly between adjacent posts.

The other, less obtrusive, way of protecting conifers from "wind-burn" is to use an anti-desiccant product. Spray this thoroughly all over each plant, following the manufacturer's instructions, and it should protect them for about 2 weeks. Repeat the application if necessary.

Mulch between the plants, if required, with a layer of bark chippings, peat or well-rotted manure or garden compost.

The following year, in **spring**, when the plants begin to grow again, topdress the soil in the bed with 1–2 inches of compost, leaf mold, or well-rotted manure. Work the organic matter into the soil, taking care to avoid damaging any plant roots. Unless your soil has unusual nutrient deficiencies, this annual top dressing should provide all the food the plants need for good growth. It is important to avoid overfertilizing conifers, as this will cause them to put out rapid, weak growth.

Mulch the entire conifer bed with a new dressing of straw or bark chips. Be sure the soil is moist before mulching. Hoe or hand weed the bed first to remove weeds.

Remove any stakes that were provided to support tall conifers. The plants should be well established.

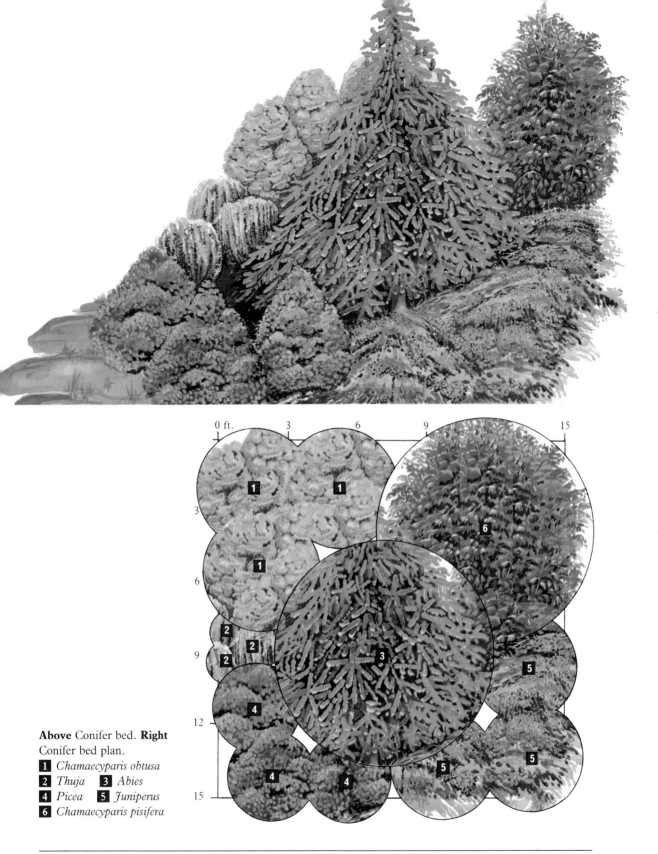

Above Conifer bed. **Right**
Conifer bed plan.
1 *Chamaecyparis obtusa*
2 *Thuja* **3** *Abies*
4 *Picea* **5** *Juniperus*
6 *Chamaecyparis pisifera*

(Mid spring)

Fork over the bottom of the hole to loosen the soil and, without breaking up the rootball, stand the plant in it. Now check to see that the soil mark on the stem matches up with the new level of soil around it. If the plant is too high or low in the ground, dig it up and start again. When the level is correct, fill in around the rootball with soil and firm down all around the plant with your foot.

Water the conifers, giving each plant about ½ gallon of water.

> **In subsequent years**, prune picea very lightly with hedging shears to give the plants a good conical shape just before they put on their burst of growth. Needles cut in half by pruning will then soon disappear under the new layer of growth.
>
> Prune conifers that are growing out of shape just to restore their appearance.

Late spring

Hoe or hand weed regularly every week if mulching was not done to ensure new plants do not become smothered by weeds.

Water newly planted conifers whenever the soil is dry, as they turn brown if they lack moisture. Usually the base of the plant turns brown first, but in very dry conditions the whole plant can go brown.

The best way to avoid this happening is to check the soil every week by digging down to the depth of a trowel and feeling if the soil is moist at that level.

> **The following year**, make sure you keep the conifers well watered in dry spells to enable them to make the most of their maximum growth period.
>
> **In subsequent years**, the plants will spread to cover the ground in the bed. You can then discontinue mulching or weeding; the shade cast by the plants will prevent weeds from germinating.

Throughout summer

Continue to weed and water regularly during the summer.

Early autumn

Pruning is not generally needed as the type of conifers used in this garden are slow growing. If, however, a branch happens to become broken or grow out of shape, it is best to cut it right back to its junction with a main branch. Avoid snipping little bits here and there, or leaving short stumps which can often become infected with plant diseases later. Now is a good time to do this job as conifers may undergo a second short flush of growth in autumn, and you should ideally do any pruning or trimming just before it starts.

Gold

Gold foliage is used in various shades to create a bed with a distinctive and bright appearance. For the plants in the original plan, substitute the following.

Mid spring

30 *Thuja orientalis* 'Aurea'

2 *Chamaecyparis pisifera* 'Filifera Aurea'

16 *Thuja occidentalis* 'Rheingold'

1 *Chamaecyparis obtusa* 'Tetragona Aurea'

From the garden shed

You will also need seaweed fertilizer

1 *Thuja orientalis*   **2** *Chamaecyparis pisifera*
3 *Thuja occidentalis*   **4** *Chamaecyparis obtusa*

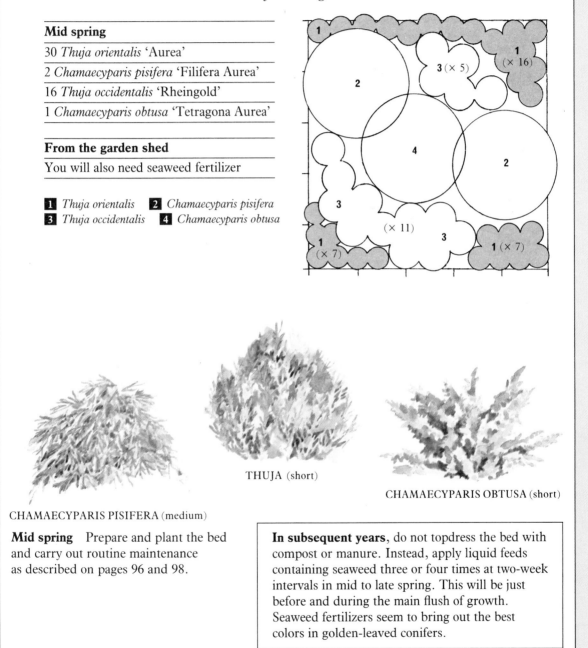

CHAMAECYPARIS PISIFERA (medium)

THUJA (short)

CHAMAECYPARIS OBTUSA (short)

Mid spring   Prepare and plant the bed and carry out routine maintenance as described on pages 96 and 98.

In subsequent years, do not topdress the bed with compost or manure. Instead, apply liquid feeds containing seaweed three or four times at two-week intervals in mid to late spring. This will be just before and during the main flush of growth. Seaweed fertilizers seem to bring out the best colors in golden-leaved conifers.

Emphasizing Form

This variation uses plants that demonstrate the architectural characteristics of conifers. You will need the following plants in place of those in the original plan.

Mid spring

8 *Picea glauca* 'Conica'

1 *Chamaecyparis lawsoniana* 'Ellwoodii'

3 *Cedrus libani* 'Sargentii'

1 *Tsuga canadensis* 'Pendula'

2 *Chamaecyparis obtusa* 'Nana'

2 *Juniperus horizontalis*

3 *Pinus sylvestris* 'Watereri'

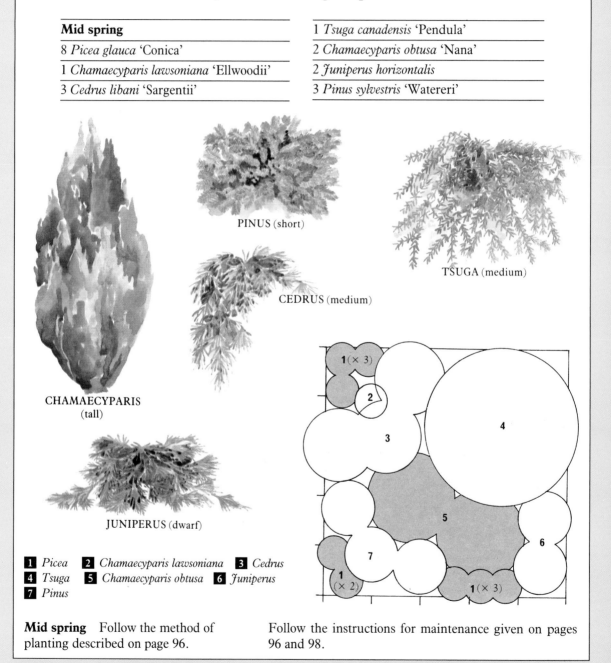

PINUS (short)

TSUGA (medium)

CEDRUS (medium)

CHAMAECYPARIS
(tall)

JUNIPERUS (dwarf)

1 *Picea* **2** *Chamaecyparis lawsoniana* **3** *Cedrus*
4 *Tsuga* **5** *Chamaecyparis obtusa* **6** *Juniperus*
7 *Pinus*

Mid spring Follow the method of planting described on page 96.

Follow the instructions for maintenance given on pages 96 and 98.

Low-Growing

The main plan and both the previous variations included plants which will lend height to the bed to create a contrast with lower-growing plants. This variation concentrates entirely on low-growing conifers. This makes the design particularly suitable for use as a ground cover planting or to create a foreground to some other feature in the garden that you might wish to emphasize. It could, for instance, be used in front of a house to add character to a particularly dramatic frontage or a long sweeping drive. It would also enhance a backdrop of taller specimen trees or a wall covered in climbers. Use the following plants to replace those listed in our original plan.

Mid spring

6 *Juniperus sabina* 'Tamariscifolia'

3 *Juniperus squamata* 'Meyeri'

5 *Thuja orientalis* 'Aurea'

4 *Juniperus horizontalis*

2 *Pinus sylvestris* 'Watereri'

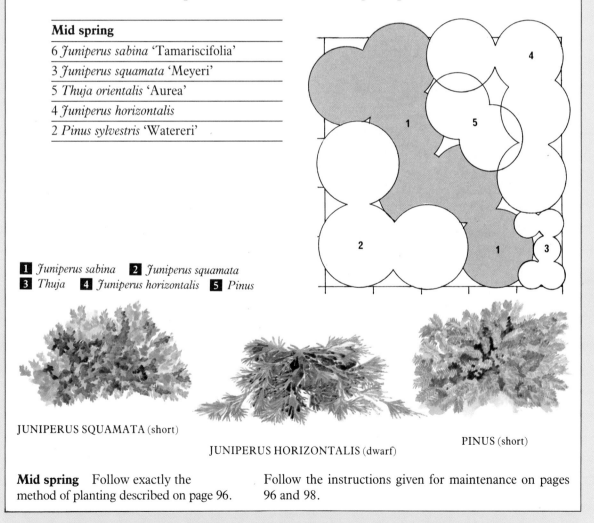

1 *Juniperus sabina*　**2** *Juniperus squamata*
3 *Thuja*　**4** *Juniperus horizontalis*　**5** *Pinus*

JUNIPERUS SQUAMATA (short)

JUNIPERUS HORIZONTALIS (dwarf)

PINUS (short)

Mid spring   Follow exactly the method of planting described on page 96.

Follow the instructions given for maintenance on pages 96 and 98.

With Ground Cover

This final variation includes evergreen ground cover plants and a variety of foliage textures. Use the following plants:

Mid spring

6 *Erica carnea* 'Pink Spangles'

6 *Erica carnea* 'Springwood White'

1 *Abies koreana*

5 *Cotoneaster horizontalis*

5 *Genista pilosa* 'Vancouver Gold'

1 *Chamaecyparis lawsoniana* 'Ellwoodii'

1 *Chamaecyparis obtusa* 'Nana'

From the garden shed

About 2½ yards flexible wire, to cut into 8 inch lengths

CHAMAECYPARIS (tall)

ERICA (dwarf) 'Pink Spangles'

ERICA (dwarf) 'Springwood White'

ABIES (tall)

1 *Erica* 'Pink Spangles': Late winter–mid spring **2** *Erica* 'Springwood White': Late winter–mid spring **3** *Abies*
4 *Cotoneaster*: Early summer (flowers); autumn (red berries) **5** *Genista*: Late spring–early summer **6** *Chamaecyparis lawsoniana* **7** *Chamaecyparis obtusa*

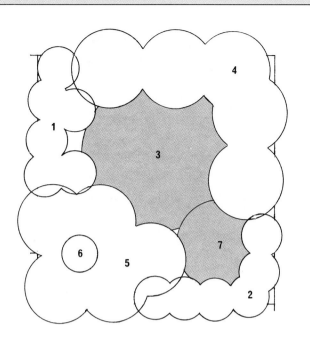

Replacement and additional plants are given at the start of each variation. For quantities of original plants, uncolored in the planting plan and not given in the variation ingredients, check with the list at the start of the main plan.

Mid spring Prepare the ground and plant the abies and chamaecyparis as described on page 96. Plant the erica, cotoneaster and genista at the same time, following exactly the same method.

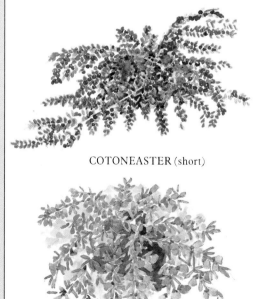

COTONEASTER (short)

GENISTA (short)

Late spring When the flowers of erica are over, clip the plants lightly with hedging shears to remove the dead flowers and reshape them slightly. Do not cut them back hard.

In subsequent years, repeat the clipping of erica annually; this way you should never need to do any drastic reshaping of the plants, but if harder pruning is required, avoid cutting into the old wood near the base of the plants as this may kill them.

Do not prune or clip genista – the plants grow into a very pleasing shape without it, and it can in fact be harmful to them.

Throughout summer Early in June, cut back late-flowering erica as described above.

Peg down the shoots of cotoneaster with pieces of bent wire formed into "hairpins". This is to hold them in place as they grow, encouraging them to spread as widely as possible over the space allocated to them.

Shrub Borders

Shrubs are among the most varied and colorful plants in the garden, offering a wide range of attractions right around the year without taking much time or work to look after. They offer flowers, berries, evergreen foliage, autumn tints, colored leaves and scented flowers, making them an ideal choice for a constantly changing focal area in the garden.

Shrubs take time to become established, so much of the maintenance is in subsequent years, rather than in the first year of planting.

Ingredients for a border 15 foot × 15 foot

Mid spring

3 *Mahonia aquifolium*
1 *Berberis thunbergii* 'Atropurpurea'
3 *Azalea* 'Elizabeth'
6 *Cotoneaster horizontalis*
3 *Genista pilosa* 'Vancouver Gold'
1 *Viburnum tinus*
1 *Kerria japonica* 'Pleniflora'
5 *Spiraea × bumalda* 'Gold Flame'

From the garden shed

12 × 2 gallon bucketfuls of bark chips or garden compost for mulching (optional)
4–6 pounds 5–10–5 or 4–12–4 fertilizer
2 × 2 gallon bucketfuls of peat moss

Tools required

Spade
Garden fork
Rake
Garden line
Hand trowel
Watering can or hose and lawn sprinkler
Pruning shears
Hoe (optional)

KERRIA (medium)

Method

Choose a site that is sunny or partly shaded for your shrub bed. It should ideally receive direct sunlight for at least half the day. The bed should be cut into a lawn, as the plan is for an island garden which has been designed to be viewed from all sides. Being a formal shape, the bed will look best if it is aligned to run parallel with any existing straight features in the garden, such as the side of the house, the garden fence or a path. However, the same design could be easily adapted to make a "teardrop"-shaped bed, which could be tailored into a contour in the ground to suit a less formal garden.

Mark out the bed with a garden line or four stakes and a ball of string. Cut out, using the spade the wrong way round so that it enters the soil at right angles to it, giving a neat edge.

Prepare the soil as described in the introduction.

Most shrubs are sold in pots, but some are balled and burlapped, that is they come with a ball of soil round their roots, wrapped in burlap.

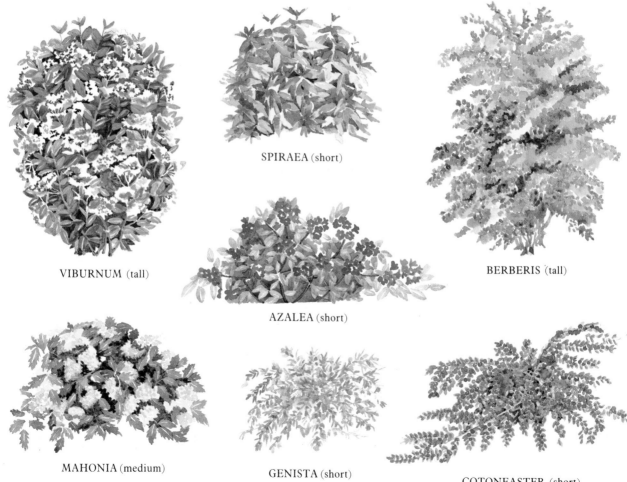

VIBURNUM (tall)

SPIRAEA (short)

AZALEA (short)

BERBERIS (tall)

MAHONIA (medium)

GENISTA (short)

COTONEASTER (short)
(winter)

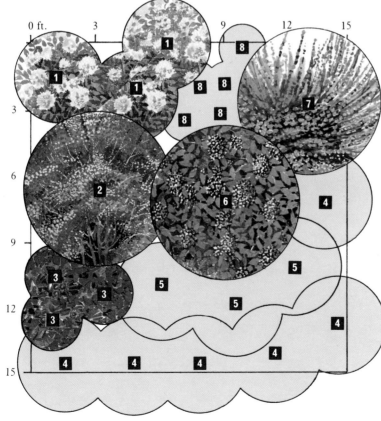

Above Shrub border. **Left** Plan for the border. Colored areas indicate shrubs in flower in spring. Average flowering periods are listed below:
1 *Mahonia*: Early to mid spring **2** *Berberis*: Mid spring; autumn and winter (berries) **3** *Azaleas*: Mid spring **4** *Cotoneaster*: Summer (flowers); autumn (red berries) **5** *Genista*: Late spring–early summer **6** *Viburnum*: Mid spring **7** *Kerria*: Mid spring **8** *Spiraea*: Late spring–mid summer

Mid spring

Before planting Give plants in containers a thorough watering and let them stand for 12 hours. If you are using balled and burlapped plants, untie the wrappings and soak the roots in a bucket of water for an hour. Try not to remove any soil from around the roots. Then stand the shrubs in their positions on the bed next to the marker stakes, turning them so that their best side faces towards the edge of the bed.

Planting Plant container-grown shrubs by digging a hole big enough to take the pot, leaving its rim level with the surrounding soil. Fork over the soil at the bottom of the hole to loosen it. When planting azaleas, mix in one 2 gallon bucketful of peat moss.

Next, if the plant is in a rigid pot knock it out, giving the bottom of the pot a sharp tap with the handle of the trowel. If the pot is thin plastic, cut it away, being careful not to slice into the rootball.

Check the base of the rootball; if it is a mass of tightly coiled roots, gently tease a few of these out.

Stand the plant in the hole, facing the outside of the bed, then fill in round the roots with soil. Finally, firm down around the rootball with your foot.

To plant balled and burlapped shrubs, dig a hole slightly wider than the rootball and about the same depth. Fork over the bottom of the hole to loosen the soil; when planting azaleas, mix one 2 gallon bucketful of peat moss into the soil at the bottom of the planting hole at this stage.

Without breaking the rootball up, stand the plant in the hole. Make sure it is level with the surrounding soil surface.

Water the new shrubs in, giving each one about 1 gallon of water.

MAINTENANCE

Mulch the entire surface of the bed, if required, with a layer of bark chips or garden compost.

Whether you mulch the bed or not, it is essential to mulch the azaleas with peat. Apply a bucketful in a circle about 12 inches wide around the plant. If your soil is not naturally slightly acid, use peat moss, which is acid.

The following year, feed the bed by scattering fertilizer evenly over the soil at 2–3 pounds per 100 square feet. Hoe the fertilizer in and water thoroughly if the soil is dry.

Mulch the bed with peat or well-rotted compost or manure.

Mulch the azaleas with a bucketful of peat moss, spreading it in a circle around the plant over an area the same diameter as that covered by the branches.

In subsequent years, repeat the annual cycle of feeding, mulching and weeding. Always mulch the azaleas with peat moss.

No regular pruning is needed for berberis, but when the plants become large you can remove a few of the oldest branches (covered with darker colored skin than the young shoots). Cut them right back to ground level, using pruning shears.

Cotoneaster stems can be pegged down now, using pieces of wire bent over to make "hairpins". This encourages them to spread over the bed and they will normally take root where they are pinned, thus growing into new plants and covering the ground very effectively. Cotoneaster can be cut back if some shoots are too long.

Azalea 'Elizabeth' does not need regular pruning; just cut out any dead or broken branches.

Mahonia should not be pruned until the end of the month, by which time the flowers are over. Regular pruning is not necessary, but when the plants get big, cut a few of the oldest branches right back to ground level to encourage the production of plenty of new young shoots.

If mahonia grows badly out of shape it can, if necessary, be cut back very hard without harm.

Mid spring

Water newly planted shrubs whenever the soil is dry. Weed regularly every 1–2 weeks, if required.

> **In subsequent years**, remove the dead flower heads of the azaleas, nipping them off between thumb and forefinger. Do not use pruning shears.
>
> Prune viburnum if necessary after the flowers are over. Remove dead or broken branches at their junction with a healthy shoot, and cut out a few of the oldest (darker) branches once the plants look overgrown. Cut them right out at the base of the plant.
>
> Prune kerria after the flowers are over. Cut out all the shoots that have flowered, right back to their junction with strong, healthy young shoots near the base of the plant. When the plant has grown large and the new shoots look overcrowded, thin them out slightly by cutting the thinnest shoots off at ground level.
>
> Weed or hoe regularly. If weeds such as thistles, nettles or docks come up in the bed pull them carefully.
>
> Water only in very dry spells.

Early and mid summer

Continue weeding regularly, by hand or using a hoe.

One important point to note is *not* to remove the dead flower heads from mahonia, berberis or cotoneaster. Do not prune or cut back genista.

Continue to water the plants whenever the soil is dry.

Late summer

Continue weeding and watering.

Late in the month, remove the dead flower heads from spiraea, using pruning shears, as soon as they are over.

25 foot × 15 foot Border

Here the same basic plan is extended by adding some extra plants for the benefit of those with larger gardens to fill. Again, the additions have been chosen to be as representative as possible of the full range of attractions shrubs have to offer. To the list of plants given in the basic plan, you will need to add the following:

Mid spring

10 *Euonymus fortunei* 'Emerald 'n' Gold'

1 *Weigela florida*

15 *Potentilla fruticosa*

3 *Lavandula spica* 'Hidcote' (lavender)

6 *Veronica incana*

1 *Cornus alba* 'Elegantissima'

1 *Cytisus × kewensis*

1 *Cotinus coggygria*

HEBE (medium) 'Great Orme'

EUONYMUS (short)

CORNUS (tall)

CYTISUS (short)

POTENTILLA (medium)

WEIGELA (medium)

COTINUS (tall)

VERONICA (short)

LAVANDULA (short)

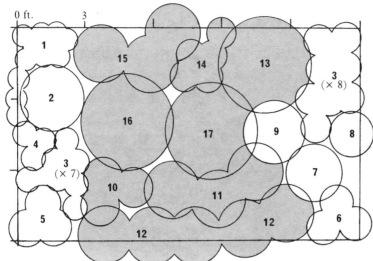

1 *Euonymus* **2** *Weigela*: Mid–late spring
3 *Potentilla*: Early–mid summer **4** *Lavender*: Mid–late summer **5** *Veronica incana*: Early–late summer **6** *Cornus*
7 *Cytisus*: Mid–late spring **8** *Cotinus* **9** *Azalea*
10 *Genista* **11** *Cotoneaster*
12 *Kerria* **13** *Spiraea*
14 *Mahonia* **15** *Berberis*
16 *Viburnum*

Mid spring Prepare the border as described on page 105, but extend its length by 10 feet. Following the method on page 107, plant the new shrubs as in the plan.

Late summer Lightly clip potentilla with hedging shears to remove the dead flowers and reshape the plants.

Mid autumn Clip lavender lightly with shears to remove the dead flower heads and reshape the plants. Never cut back into the dark-colored wood near the base of the plants.

Replacement and additional plants are given at the start of each variation. For quantities of original plants, uncolored in the planting plan and not given in the variation ingredients, check with the list at the start of the main plan.

In subsequent years, in **early spring**, cut out the oldest (dark and dull) stems of cornus, taking them right back down to ground level. Cut back veronica slightly to reshape the plants and remove damaged shoots.

Cut back long or untidy branches of cotinus to a convenient junction with another shoot. Euonymus is unlikely to need any pruning or clipping.

In **late spring**, clip cytisus lightly with shears after the flowers are over to remove the tips of the flowering shoots and tidy the plant.

In **mid summer**, cut a few old branches of weigela right down to ground level as soon as it has finished flowering each year.

In **mid autumn**, repeat the clipping of lavender annually after flowering.

Emphasizing Foliage

This variation keeps the same basic pattern as the original plan but changes the plants entirely, giving a garden where the emphasis is on foliage. For the original plants, substitute the following:

Mid spring

13 *Euonymus fortunei* 'Emerald 'n' Gold' (replace *Mahonia aquifolium* and *Spiraea × bumalda* 'Gold Flame')

1 *Cornus alba* 'Elegantissima' (replaces *Berberis thunbergii* 'Atropurpurea')

4 *Mahonia aquifolium* (replace *Azalea* 'Elizabeth' and *Genista* 'Vancouver Gold')

11 *Euonymus fortunei* 'Silver Queen' (replace *Cotoneaster horizontalis*)

1 *Cotinus coggygria* (replaces *Viburnum tinus*)

1 *Elaeagnus pungens* 'Maculata' (replaces *Kerria japonica* 'Pleniflora')

CORNUS (tall)

CORNUS (tall)
(winter)

ELAEAGNUS (tall)

EUONYMUS (medium)
'Silver Queen'

EUONYMUS (short)
'Emerald N' Gold'

COTINUS (tall)

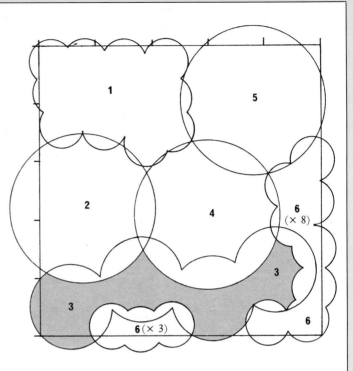

1 *Euonymus* 'Emerald 'n' Gold'
2 *Cornus*   **3** *Mahonia*   **4** *Cotinus*
5 *Elaeagnus*   **6** *Euonymus* 'Silver Queen'

Mid spring   Follow the same method as described on pages 105 and 107 for preparing the bed, planting and establishing the plants.

In subsequent years, in **early spring**, cut out all the oldest stems of cornus, taking them right back down to ground level. The old shoots can easily be recognized by the fact that their bark has lost its bright red coloring and become dark and dull. These are removed to encourage new young shoots and maintain the bright red stem color, which is particularly conspicuous in winter.

Cut back any long or untidy branches of cotinus to a convenient junction with another shoot, sufficient to tidy the plant when it becomes overgrown.

In **mid spring**, trim the euonymus 'Silver Queen' with shears every year to maintain the height at around 1–2 feet. This is best done now, at the start of the growing season, so that any leaves cut in half by the trimming are quickly covered by new growth.

Euonymus 'Emerald 'n' Gold' is unlikely to need any pruning or clipping.

In **summer**, remove any plain green shoots from the variegated evergreen elaeagnus as soon as you notice them.

Year-Round Color

This variation presents a complete change of plants while still keeping the same basic pattern of the main plan.

Mid spring

1 *Viburnum tinus* (replaces *Berberis thunbergii* 'Atropurpurea')

1 *Daphne odora* (replaces *Azalea* 'Elizabeth')

4 *Genista pilosa* 'Vancouver Gold' and
1 *Hamamelis mollis*
(replace *Cotoneaster horizontalis*)

4 *Cytisus kewensis* (replace *Genista pilosa* 'Vancouver Gold')

1 *Forsythia × intermedia* 'Spectabilis' (replaces *Viburnum tinus*)

1 *Philadelphus* 'Belle Etoile' (replaces *Kerria japonica* 'Pleniflora')

3 *Spiraea × bumalda* 'Anthony Waterer'

1 *Potentilla fruticosa*,
1 *Hypericum patulum* 'Hidcote',
1 *Hibiscus syriacus*, and
4 *Cytisus kewensis*
(replace *Spiraea × bumalda* 'Gold Flame' and *Mahonia aquifolium*)

PHILADELPHUS (tall)

DAPHNE (medium)

FORSYTHIA (tall)

POTENTILLA (medium)

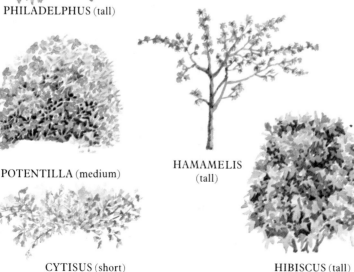

HAMAMELIS (tall)

SPIRAEA (medium)

CYTISUS (short)

HIBISCUS (tall)

HYPERICUM (medium)

1 *Viburnum* **2** *Daphne*: Late winter–early spring **3** *Genista* **4** *Cytisus*: Mid–late spring **5** *Forsythia*: Early spring **6** *Philadelphus*: Late spring–early summer **7** *Spiraea* **8** *Potentilla*: Early–mid summer **9** *Hibiscus*: Mid–late summer **10** *Hamamelis*: Late winter **11** *Hypericum*: Mid summer–early autumn

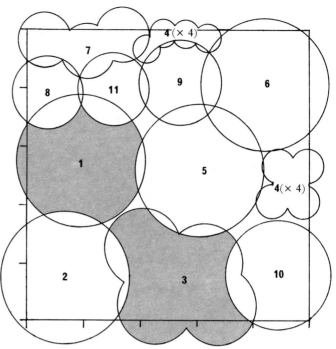

Mid spring   Follow the method described on pages 105 and 107 for preparing the bed, planting and establishing the plants.

After planting, prune back the shoots of forsythia by about half, cutting them off above a leaf joint.

In subsequent years, in **late winter**, cut back broken or straggly hamamelis stems, after flowering, cutting to their junction with another branch.

In **early spring**, prune hypericum, shortening the longest shoots to keep it in shape.

In **mid spring**, prune forsythia after flowering. Cut any damaged or dead shoots back to healthy wood and remove a few of the oldest (darker) branches back to the junction with a main branch or ground level.

In **late spring**, clip cytisus with shears after flowering to remove tips of flowering shoots.

In **mid summer**, prune philadelphus after the flowers are over. Cut out some of the oldest shoots each year to their junction with another branch.

In **late summer**, clip potentilla with hedging shears after flowering to remove the dead heads.

Clip the dead flower heads from the spiraea.

In **early winter** hibiscus requires no regular pruning; just shorten long shoots immediately after flowering.

Fragrant

The final variation on the shrub theme concentrates on creating an area of garden which will be rich in fragrance. For the plants in the original plan, substitute the following:

Mid spring

3 *Chaenomeles speciosa*, and
7 *Lavandula spica* 'Hidcote' (lavender)
(replace *Mahonia aquifolium*)

1 *Philadelphus* 'Belle Etoile' (replaces *Berberis thunbergii* 'Atropurpurea')

1 *Daphne odora* 'Aureomarginata'

15 *Lavandula spica* 'Hidcote' (lavender)

1 *Hamamelis mollis* and
1 *Rosa* 'Boule de Neige'
(replace *Azalea* 'Elizabeth', *Cotoneaster horizontalis* and *Genista pilosa* 'Vancouver Gold')

1 *Buddleia davidii* (replaces *Viburnum tinus*)

1 *Viburnum farreri* (replaces *Kerria japonica* 'Pleniflora')

1 *Rosmarinus officinalis* (replaces *Spiraea × bumalda* 'Gold Flame')

ROSA (tall)

VIBURNUM (tall)

BUDDLEIA (tall)

LAVANDULA (short)

ROSMARINUS (tall)

CHAENOMELES (medium)

HAMAMELIS (tall)

PHILADELPHUS (tall)

DAPHNE (medium)

Mid spring   Prepare and plant the bed in exactly the same way as described on page 107.

Summer   Deadhead the rose regularly, cutting back to the next full size leaf down the stem.

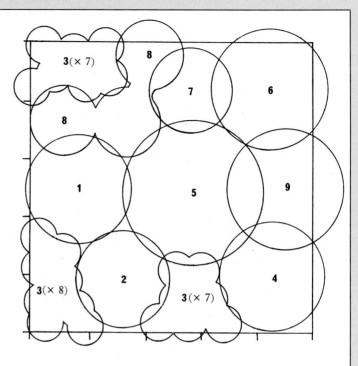

1 *Philadelphus*: Late spring–early summer
2 *Daphne*: Early spring   3 *Lavender*:
Mid–late summer   4 *Rose*: Early
summer–early autumn   5 *Buddleia*:
Summer–autumn   6 *Viburnum*: Mid–
spring   7 *Rosemary*   8 *Chaenomeles*:
Mid spring   9 *Hamamelis*: Late winter

In subsequent years, in **late winter**, cut back broken or straggly hamamelis stems to another branch.

In **early spring**, cut buddleia shoots that flowered the previous year down to within 6–8 inches of the dark, older wood.

Prune rose 'Boule de Neige' by cutting away weak, twiggy shoots and dead growth.

In **mid spring**, cut out dead, damaged or overcrowded viburnum branches after flowering. Cut out dead or browning shoots of rosemary, and shorten tall branches.

In **late spring**, thin out overcrowded chaenomeles branches by cutting back to another branch after flowering.

In **late summer**, cut some of the oldest philadelphus shoots to another branch after flowering. Daphne is not pruned.

In **mid autumn**, clip lavender with shears to remove dead flowers and reshape the plant.

In **late autumn**, prune rose 'Boule de Neige' after flowering: cut out dead, damaged or weak shoots and shorten tips of shoots slightly to remove soft growth before winter.

Dry, Sunny Beds

How do you turn a "problem" dry border into an easily maintained and attractive feature that will grace any garden? The secret lies in using plants that actually prefer dry living conditions, instead of struggling to grow "ordinary" garden plants in places that don't suit them. Then, using a pleasing design, you can easily create an unusual and stylish border. The main plan here makes the most of a hot, dry area by converting it into a Mediterranean border that will act as a permanent reminder of holidays in the sun.

Ingredients for a dry, sunny border 15 foot × 4 foot

Early to mid spring

1 *Rosmarinus officinalis* (rosemary)

1 *Juniperus squamata* 'Meyeri' (juniper)

3 *Perovskia atriplicifolia*

1 *Santolina chamaecyparissus*

1 *Senecio* 'Sunshine'

6 *Dianthus* 'Doris'

2 *Helianthemum nummularium*

8 *Iberis umbellata* 'Giant Hyacinth'

3 *Lavandula spica* 'Hidcote' (lavender)

From the garden shed

Slug traps and bait if necessary

30 × 2 gallon bucketfuls of gravel or marble chips (optional)

Tools required

Spade

Garden fork

Rake

Garden line

Hand trowel

Watering can or hose

Pruning shears

Method

Choose a sunny but reasonably well-sheltered site, and mark out a rectangle 15 foot long by 4 foot wide, using a garden line. Cut alongside the line with a spade to form the boundary of the bed. Use the spade the wrong way around so that the blade goes into the soil vertically, giving a nice clean edge which can easily be kept tidy. Now take away the line, and prepare the soil as described in the introduction.

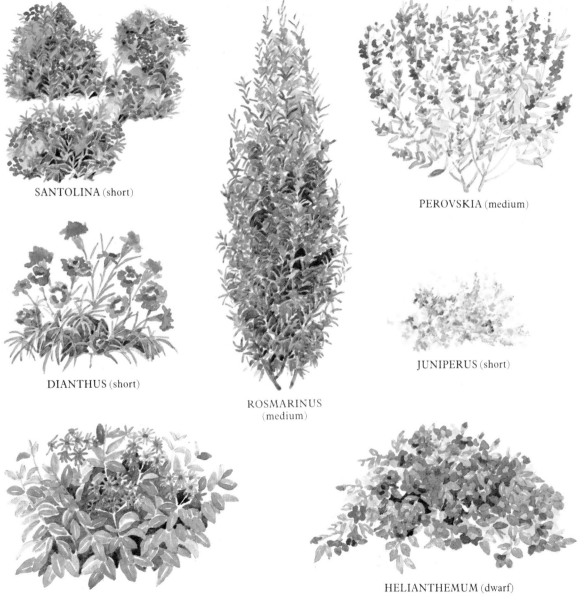

SANTOLINA (short)

PEROVSKIA (medium)

DIANTHUS (short)

ROSMARINUS
(medium)

JUNIPERUS (short)

SENECIO (short)

HELIANTHEMUM (dwarf)

Early to mid spring

Planting   To plant the rosemary, juniper, perovskia, santolina, senecio, dianthus, helianthemum and lavender, check with the plan and stand them, still in their pots, roughly in position. Turn each plant so that its "best" side faces the front of the border.

Start planting from the back of the bed, lifting each pot in turn and marking its exact position with the trowel. Dig a small hole the same depth as the pot in the position you have marked and gently knock the plant out by tapping the base of its pot with the trowel. Taking great care not to break up the ball of roots, place the plant into its hole. The top of the rootball should now be level with the surface of the surrounding soil. If it is not, add or subtract a little soil from the bottom of the hole to level it up. Double check that the best side of the plant is still facing the front and fill in around the roots with soil. Finish by firming the soil down lightly around the plant using the handle of the trowel.

MAINTENANCE

The day after planting, check the iberis to see if they need watering again.

Once a week, check all the plants in the bed and water them if the soil is very dry.

(Early to mid spring)

To plant the iberis just peel the container away if it is the flexible sort or, if it is rigid, loosen the plants by tapping the tray down on a hard surface once or twice. You can then simply tip them out. Separate each plant from the solid mass of roots by tearing them carefully apart, leaving them with a roughly equal-sized ball of roots. Lay them out in position and, as you come to plant, lift each in turn and mark its position with a trowel. Dig a hole about 1 inch deeper than each rootball and plant so that the tops of the roots are slightly below the surface of the soil.

When you have laid out the whole bed, water each plant in with a watering can or hose. Give the rosemary, juniper, lavender, perovskia, santolina and senecio approximately ½ gallon of water each, and the iberis, helianthemum and dianthus about 1 pint each.

To finish the bed, apply a layer of gravel or marble chips all over the surface of the bed as a top-dressing, at the rate of two bucketfuls of chippings per running yard of bed. This is not essential and can be left out if you prefer, but it looks very ornamental and is very beneficial too, helping to smother germinating weed seedlings and retain moisture in the soil.

If slugs are a problem in your garden, set out traps between the iberis plants.

Opposite Dry, sunny bed. **Below** Plan for the bed. Colored areas indicate plants in flower in mid summer. Average flowering periods are listed below: **1** *Rosemary* **2** *Juniper* **3** *Perovskia*: Late summer–early autumn **4** *Santolina*: Mid–late summer **5** *Senecio*: Early–mid summer **6** *Dianthus*: Early–mid summer **7** *Helianthemum*: Early–mid summer **8** *Iberis*: Late spring–late summer **9** *Lavender*: Mid–late summer

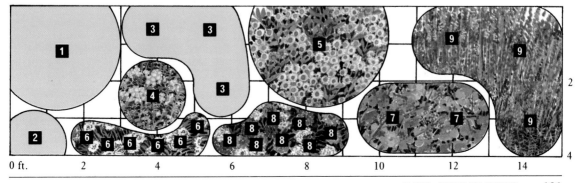

(Early to mid spring)

In subsequent years, cut back any shoots of rosemary that have been damaged by cold weather or wind during the winter. Cut back a whole shoot at a time right to the point where it originates from a main branch.

If santolina or senecio become overgrown, this is the time to cut back the untidy shoots to their base.

Lavender can also be pruned lightly now, but avoid cutting back into the dark old wood from which it is difficult for new shoots to regenerate. Cut broken or awkwardly shaped juniper branches back to a main branch or the stem.

Use pruning shears for all these jobs. Give the entire bed its annual feeding. Scatter the fertilizer evenly over the soil surface and hoe it lightly in.

Plant new iberis as before and water them in.

Follow up by applying more gravel or marble chips if the previous layer is looking thin. You will need very much less material now than you used in the first place and 7–8 bucketfuls should be sufficient.

Late spring

Continue to check all the plants and water if the soil is dry.

Mid summer

Using pruning shears, cut the faded flower heads from dianthus. They will then sometimes go on to produce a second flush of flowers later. Cut back the helianthemum after flowering to remove the tips of the shoots complete with dead flowers, and encourage a second flowering in late summer or early autumn. Water the juniper in dry weather to prevent foliage from browning.

Early autumn

Pull out the iberis plants when they are finished blooming. Use pruning shears to clip off the dead flower heads from lavender and santolina and lightly trim the plants into compact, bushy shapes.

Use pruning shears to remove the dead flower heads from perovskia and senecio. This is just to tidy the bushes; do not actually prune them now.

Rosemary, being slow growing, will not need pruning, but cut out entirely, with the pruning shears, any shoots that have become broken, or which are starting to spoil the shape of the plant by growing out at odd angles.

Dry and Shady

This variation is for a different type of dry site – this time a shady one. By including evergreens and spring bulbs, it looks good all year round. It also requires very little maintenance. Buy the plants listed here in place of those shown in brackets.

Early spring

1 *Berberis thunbergii* 'Atropurpurea' (replaces *Perovskia atriplicifolia* and *Santolina chamaecyparissus*)

1 *Sambucus canadensis* 'Aurea' (replaces *Senecio* 'Sunshine')

3 *Polygonum affine* (replace *Dianthus* 'Doris')

3 *Salvia superba* 'East Friesland' (replace *Iberis umbellata* 'Giant Hyacinth' and 1 *Helianthemum nummularium*)

1 *Bergenia cordifolia* (replaces 1 *Helianthemum nummularium*)

1 *Alchemilla mollis* (replaces 1 *Lavandula spica* 'Hidcote')

1 *Cotoneaster dammeri* 'Skogholm' (replaces 2 *Lavandula spica* 'Hidcote')

Mid spring

1 *Elaeagnus pungens* 'Maculata' (replaces *Rosmarinus officinalis*)

5 *Ajuga reptans* (replace *Juniperus squamata* 'Meyeri')

Early autumn

30 *Anemone blanda* (replace *Juniperus squamata* 'Meyeri')

From the garden shed

Substitute bark chips for stone, for a classic shade-garden finish

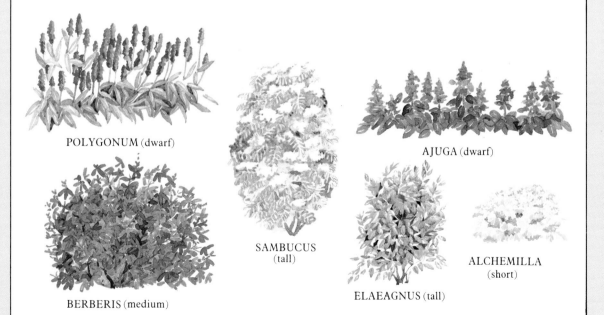

POLYGONUM (dwarf)

SAMBUCUS (tall)

AJUGA (dwarf)

BERBERIS (medium)

ELAEAGNUS (tall)

ALCHEMILLA (short)

SALVIA
(short)

BERGENIA (short)

COTONEASTER
(tall)

ANEMONE
(dwarf)

Early spring   Plant out the berberis, sambucus, polygonum, salvia, bergenia, cotoneaster and alchemilla following instructions for rosemary etc on page 120.

Mid spring   Plant out the elaeagnus and ajuga following the instructions for rosemary etc on page 120.

> Replacement and additional plants are given at the start of each variation. For quantities of original plants, uncolored in the planting plan and not given in the variation ingredients, check with the list at the start of the main plan.

Early autumn   Plant the anemone corms. Dig holes 3 inches deep evenly spaced among the ajuga. Drop a corm into each hole and fill with soil.

> **In subsequent years**, in **mid spring**, deadhead anemones and cut dead foliage to ground level.
>   Shorten long straggling shoots on the elaeagnus, using pruning shears. Cut damaged or dead sambucus shoots back to a healthy shoot. Shorten overlong cotoneaster branches. Cut back tips of berberis shoots that don't produce new buds when the rest of the plant does.

Early summer   Keep the bed free of weeds. Snip off the dead flower heads from bergenia.

Mid summer   Remove dead heads from ajuga by clipping lightly over the plant with shears.
   Cut back dead flower stems and old foliage only of alchemilla. Late in the season cut down and remove dead flower stems and foliage from the polygonum.

Late autumn   Cut the salvia down to ground level.

1 *Elaeagnus*   **2** *Ajuga*: Early–mid summer   **3** *Anemones*: Early–mid spring   **4** *Berberis*   **5** *Sambucus*: Mid summer   **6** *Polygonum*: Mid summer   **7** *Salvia*   **8** *Bergenia*: Mid–late spring   **9** *Alchemilla*: Early–late summer   **10** *Cotoneaster*: Mid autumn–early winter (berries)

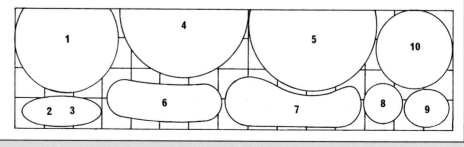

Exposed

Yet another "difficult" site. Here it is planted with a scheme designed to cope with the worst of wind and weather yet still look attractive. Substitute the plants shown here for those in brackets from the original dry border plan.

Early spring

1 *Spiraea × bumalda* 'Anthony Waterer' (replaces *Rosmarinus officinalis*)

4 *Scabiosa caucasica* (scabious), and 3 *Polygonum affine* (replace *Perovskia atriplicifolia*, *Santolina chamaecyparissus* and *Dianthus* 'Doris')

1 *Berberis thunbergii* 'Atropurpurea' (replaces *Lavandula spica* 'Hidcote')

Mid spring

1 *Euonymus fortunei* 'Silver Queen' (replaces *Senecio* 'Sunshine')

6 *Alyssum saxatile* 'Basket of Gold' (replace *Helianthemum nummularium* and *Iberis umbellata* 'Giant Hyacinth')

From the garden shed

30 × 2 gallon bucketfuls of gravel, pebbles or well-rotted manure or garden compost

$7\frac{1}{2}$ ounces sulfate of potash

EUONYMUS (medium)

ALYSSUM (dwarf)

POLYGONUM (dwarf)

BERBERIS (medium)

SCABIOSA (short)

SPIRAEA (medium)

Early spring Plant out the spiraea, scabious, polygonum and berberis following the instructions for rosemary etc on page 120.

Mid spring Plant out the euonymus and alyssum following the instructions for rosemary etc on page 120.

After planting, water the soil thoroughly and top dress with gravel, pebbles or organic material such as well-rotted manure or garden compost.

In subsequent years, reapply the top dressing to the surface of the bed as the plants are starting back into growth (7–8 bucketfuls of material). At the same time you will be able to see if there is any 'die-back' on the spiraea and berberis – tips of shoots that do not produce new buds when the rest of the plant does, showing that they have been killed by cold weather. Cut these back with pruning shears to a point where new buds are growing strongly.

Late summer Apply $1\frac{1}{2}$ ounces sulfate of potash per square yard of the soil in the bed. Water it in well. This may help to encourage the new growth to ripen, hardening it to withstand the bad weather to come.

Mid autumn Cut back and remove the dead flower stems and foliage from scabious and polygonum as soon as they start to die back naturally, using pruning shears.

Late autumn Cut alyssum and scabious stems down to ground level using pruning shears.

Prune any dead or badly browned branches of the euonymus with pruning shears right back to a main branch.

1 *Spiraea*: Late spring–mid summer **2** *Scabious*: Early summer–early autumn **3** *Polygonum*: Summer
4 *Euonymus* **5** *Alyssum*: Mid–late spring **6** *Berberis*: Late spring; autumn and winter (red berries) **7** *Juniper*

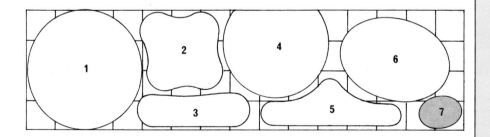

Island Bed

For something completely different, you can depart from the traditional idea of plants growing around the edges of the garden next to a hedge or fence, and instead opt for a modern alternative – an island bed. Here the plants are in the middle, with the lawn around the edge – perfect for a front garden, or in a small town garden surrounded by paving instead of grass. The great advantage of an island bed is that it not only looks striking but is easy to maintain, since you can reach all parts without having to walk on the soil. This variation uses most of the same plants as the main dry border plan, re-arranged to create an entirely different effect. You will need to buy the following additional plants:

Early spring

6 *Ajuga reptans* (extra)

4 *Polygonum affine* (extra)

Mid spring

1 *Yucca filamentosa* (replaces *Senecio* 'Sunshine')

1 *Juniperus horizontalis* 'Plumosa' (juniper) (replaces *Juniperus squamata* 'Meyeri')

From the garden shed

27 × 2 gallon bucketfuls of gravel, pebbles or bark chips (optional)

YUCCA (short)

POLYGONUM (dwarf)

AJUGA (dwarf)

JUNIPERUS (dwarf)

Mark out the bed, a circle with a diameter of 9 feet, following the instructions on page 119. For a less formal bed, elongate the shape slightly to form a "teardrop", tailored to fit into a contour in the ground for a really "designed" look. Prepare the soil as described on page 113.

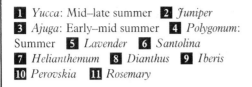

1 *Yucca*: Mid–late summer **2** *Juniper*
3 *Ajuga*: Early–mid summer **4** *Polygonum*:
Summer **5** *Lavender* **6** *Santolina*
7 *Helianthemum* **8** *Dianthus* **9** *Iberis*
10 *Perovskia* **11** *Rosemary*

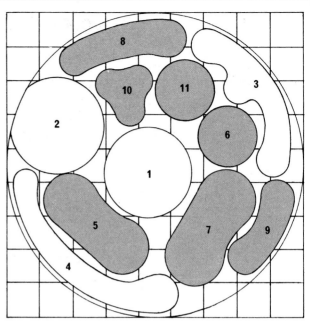

Early spring   Plant out ajuga and polygonum following instructions for rosemary etc on page 120.

Mid spring   Plant out the juniper following the instructions for rosemary etc on page 120. If winters are severe in your area leave the yucca in its pot and plant that too. Dig a hole the same size as the pot, and sink it up to its rim in the ground. After planting and watering spread bark chips, gravel or pebbles in a thin layer all over the bed.

In subsequent years, if the yucca is damaged by frost, prune it back hard with pruning shears until you are cutting into live healthy tissue (which will appear creamy green in color as against the brown of dead tissue). Cut broken or awkwardly shaped juniper branches back to a main branch or stem.

Mid summer   Clip lightly over ajuga with shears to remove dead flower heads.

Early autumn   Use pruning shears to cut back and remove the dead flower stems and foliage from the polygonum.

Mid autumn   Dig the yucca out, still in its pot, and put it in a frost-free greenhouse or porch until May or June. If you planted your yucca in the ground, give it protection in very frosty or windy weather by gathering up its leaves and tying them together with strips of old fabric. This can only be done for a week or two at a time, or the leaves may turn yellow or drop off. Another means of winter protection is a thick layer of loose mulch.

With Annuals

The final variation adds colorful annual flowers to the basic plan to bring a touch of seasonal variation to the dry border. In subsequent years you may like to add ideas of your own – it is easy to experiment with annuals, using them to provide a very different look.

Late spring

Buy the following additional plants:

8 *Osteospermum* 'Tetra Polestar' (replace *Santolina chamaecyparissus* and 1 of 3 *Perovskia atriplicifolia*)

7 *Tagetes patula* 'Suzy Wong' (French marigold) (replace *Dianthus* 'Doris' and 1 of 2 *Helianthemum nummularium*)

8 *Mesembryanthemum* 'Magic Carpet Mixed' (replace 1 of the 3 *Lavandula spica* and 1 *Helianthemum nummularium*)

From the garden shed

6 × 2 gallon bucketfuls of peat moss

MESEMBRYANTHEMUM (dwarf)

TAGETES (dwarf)

1 *Osteospermum*: Mid summer–early autumn
2 *Tagetes*: Early summer–early autumn
3 *Mesembryanthemum*: Early summer–early autumn
4 Rosemary 5 *Juniper*
6 Perovskia 7 Iberis 8 Lavender 9 Senecio

OSTEOSPERMUM
(short)

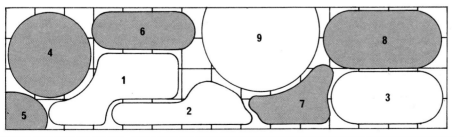

Method

Prepare and plant the bed in exactly the same way as described in the basic plan on page 119. After raking the soil and marking it out, spread 2 bucketfuls of peat moss per square yard over the areas where the osteospermum, marigolds and mesembryanthemum are to be planted, and fork it lightly into the top 3–4 inches of soil. This is to provide a moisture reserve to help them get established, as they are very shallow rooted.

Late spring Plant out the osteospermum, marigolds and mesembryanthemum following the instructions for iberis on page 121. Make quite sure that the mesembryanthemums are planted so that they receive the maximum sun possible, without being shaded by other plants, as their flowers only open when the sun is on them. Water each plant in with about 1 pint water.

Early to mid summer Water all the plants whenever the soil around them is dry for the first 8 weeks to help them get established. Throughout summer use the pruning shears to snip the dead flower heads from marigolds and osteospermum as soon as they are faded. This will encourage them to continue producing new flowers right up to the end of the summer. Do not bother to deadhead mesembryanthemum; the individual flowers only last 1–2 days each and the plants continue flowering prolifically regardless.

Early to mid autumn When the marigolds, osteospermum and mesembryanthemum have stopped producing any new flowers pull them out and throw them away.

Summer Borders

Want a colorful border in an instant? This summer bedding scheme, suitable for a sunny bed backed by a hedge, fence or wall, will give you just that. By planting annuals in summer when they are already coming into flower, you can be sure of a flower-packed bed in a matter of days. Perfect if you have just moved to a new house, or have a special occasion like a family wedding when you want to make the garden look especially colorful. Ideal, too, for people who just like to ring the changes, and try something new every year!

Ingredients for a sunny border 10 foot × 3 foot

Early to mid spring

Packet *Reseda odorata* (mignonette) seeds

Packet *Nigella damascena* 'Miss Jekyll Blue' seeds

Late spring

8 *Nicotiana alata* 'Sensation Mixed'

2 *Amaranthus caudatus* 'Love-lies-bleeding'

15 *Lobelia erinus* 'Mrs. Clibran'

8 *Pelargonium* 'Rose Diamond'

8 *Malcolmia maritima* (Virginia stock)

8 *Petunia multiflora* 'Resisto Mixed'

From the garden shed

Slug traps and bait if necessary

9–12 ounces 5–10–5 or other all-purpose fertilizer

Small bottle of liquid foliar plant food (optional)

Tools required

Spade

Garden fork

Rake

Garden line

Hand trowel

Watering can or hose

Pruning shears or sharp scissors

Lawn shears (if bed is surrounded by grass)

Method

Mark out an oblong bed 10 foot × 3 foot with the garden line. Cut alongside the line with the spade to form the boundary of the border. Use the spade the wrong way around so the blade goes into the soil vertically – this gives you a nice clean edge to the grass in front of the bed, which can easily be kept tidy with lawn shears later. Remove the line, and prepare the soil as described in the introduction.

NIGELLA (short)

RESEDA (short)

LOBELIA (dwarf)

MALCOLMIA (dwarf)

NICOTIANA (short)

PETUNIA (dwarf)

PELARGONIUM (short)

AMARANTHUS (medium)

Early to mid spring

Planting Sow the mignonette and nigella seeds. First rake the soil in the areas indicated in the plan to a fine tilth, and make sure it is level.

Then scatter the seeds where they are to flower and rake gently.

MAINTENANCE

Mid to late spring

Thin out the mignonette and nigella seedlings to six of each: when the first pair of leaves is fully expanded, remove excess seedlings with the tips of your thumb and index finger, leaving a space of 9 inches around each remaining seedling.

Late spring

Plant out the lobelia, nicotiana, amaranthus, pelargoniums, Virginia stock and petunias. Stand the pelargoniums and amaranthus in position still in their pots, allowing about 10–12 square inches for the pelargoniums and 9 square inches for the amaranthus.

The day after planting, check to see if the surface of the soil has dried out, and if so water the plants again. Continue watering like this for the first two or three weeks, until you start to see the plants growing. This indicates that they are becoming established.

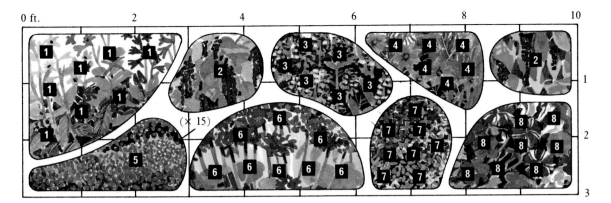

0 ft.　2　4　6　8　10

(Late spring)

Take the remaining plants out of their flats. Tear away flimsy trays but remove the rigid ones by giving the base a couple of sharp taps on a concrete pavement then tipping the contents out. Separate the plants by gently tearing the soil apart so that each of them is left with a similarly-sized rootball. Lay them in position, allowing each a space of 9 square inches. Lift each plant and mark its position with a trowel. Plant from the back of the bed to the front.

To plant the pelargoniums and amaranthus, knock them out of their pots by tapping the base with a trowel. Dig a hole the same depth as the pot, in position, then place the plant into its hole. Check the top of the rootball is level with the top of the hole. Using a trowel, fill in with soil and firm in with the trowel handle.

To plant the nicotiana, lobelia, Virginia stock and petunias, dig a hole wide enough to take the rootball and 1 inch deeper. Put the plant into the hole, with the rootball about 1 inch below the surface. Fill in with soil and lightly firm down with the trowel handle.

When you have planted the whole bed, water each plant in with approximately 1 pint of water using a watering can or hose. If slugs are a problem in your garden, set out baited slug traps.

Left Summer border **Above** Planting plan. Colored areas indicate plants in flower in mid summer. Average flowering periods are listed below. **1** *Nicotiana*: Mid–late summer **2** *Amaranthus*: Early summer–early autumn **3** *Mignonette*: Mid–late summer **4** *Nigella*: Early–late summer **5** *Lobelia*: Early–late summer **6** *Pelargonium*: Early–late summer **7** *Malcolmia*: Early–mid summer **8** *Petunias*: Early summer–early autumn

Special note

When your garden is newly planted, you must make sure that your plants receive sufficient watering. This is particularly important in the case of bedding plants which, being shallow-rooted, are very vulnerable to the top layer of soil drying out. After about a month, when the roots have penetrated deeper into the soil, looking at the surface of the soil is no longer enough. Stick your finger or the probe of an electronic water meter into the soil to a depth of 3–4 inches. If you are still unsure, dig out a handful of soil to the depth of the trowel and inspect it for moisture.

Early summer

Water every few days in dry weather and about once a week if there is some natural rainfall.

An occasional foliar feeding works wonders to "boost" a good display of flowers. Choose a cool day, or wait till late evening to apply the food. Plants must have previously been watered so that they are not under stress when you feed them, nor should the sun be on them. Dilute the food according to the manufacturer's instructions and apply it through a fine rose on a watering can or with a sprayer.

If you have set out slug traps, inspect them every few days and add bait as necessary.

Go over the bed once a week snipping off the dead flower heads with pruning shears, to encourage new blooms. Cut as closely as possible beneath the head. Remove the dead flower heads from the bed, or they may encourage pests or become a source of disease.

Hand weed the bed every two weeks to keep it tidy and weed-free. If you prefer to use a hoe, be very careful as annuals have very soft stems and are easily cut into or broken right off by careless hoeing. If the bed is set in a lawn trim the grass around the edge regularly. Each time you mow the grass, cut neatly around the edge of the border with lawn shears to give a clean finish.

Mid summer

Continue watering, feeding, weeding, deadheading and checking slug traps as above.

Late summer–early autumn

Continue weeding, watering, feeding and deadheading regularly until the plants stop producing new flowers.

Once the last flowers are finished blooming pull them out, remove any weeds from the bed and fork it over to leave it tidy for winter.

Color Contrasts

If you like sharp contrasts and strong colors, this border has been created specially for you. Gone are the subtle blends of mixed varieties, and in their place are bright, hot colors grouped to create maximum impact. For this design, you will need the following additional plants which replace those shown in brackets.

Late spring

8 *Tagetes erecta* 'Gold Galore' (African marigold) (replace *Nicotiana alata* 'Sensation Mixed')

1 *Amaranthus caudatus* 'Viridis' (replaces one of the two *Amaranthus caudatus*)

8 *Pelargonium* 'Scarlet Diamond' (replace *Pelargonium* 'Rose Diamond')

4 *Rudbeckia hirta* 'Rustic Dwarfs' (replace *Reseda odorata*)

6 *Tagetes* 'Naughty Marietta' (replace *Malcolmia maritima*)

8 *Petunia* 'White Magic' (replace *Petunia multiflora* 'Resisto Mixed')

RUDBECKIA (short)

AMARANTHUS (medium)

TAGETES ERECTA (dwarf)

PELARGONIUM (short)

PETUNIA (dwarf)

TAGETES PATULA (dwarf)

Late spring   Plant the marigolds, amaranthus, pelargonium, rudbeckia and petunias following the instructions for pelargoniums etc on page 135.

Early and mid summer   Go over the bed once a week snipping off the dead flower heads to encourage new blooms; cut just below the flower heads. Hand weed the bed every two weeks, and trim the grass around the edge of the bed with shears, if it is set in a lawn.

Late summer, early autumn   When the last flowers are over pull the plants out and throw them away. Fork over the bed and leave it tidy for winter.

1 *Tagetes* 'Gold Galore': Early summer–early autumn
2 *Amaranthus candatus* 'Viridis': Early summer–early autumn
3 *Nigella*   **4** *Amaranthus caudatus*   **5** *Lobelia*
6 *Pelargonium*: Early–late summer   **7** *Petunias*: Early–late summer   **8** *Rudbeckia*: Mid summer–early autumn
9 *Tagetes* 'Naughty Marietta': Early summer–early autumn

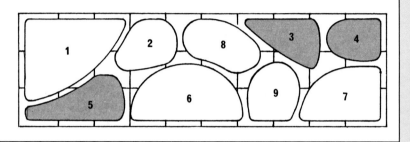

Color Harmony

This variation comes at the opposite end of the spectrum to the previous one as far as mood is concerned. Instead of using strong colors to make lively contrasts, it employs gentle harmonies of color to create a border that is quiet and relaxing in character. Buy the following plants to replace those shown in brackets.

Early to mid spring

Packet *Godetia grandiflora* seeds (replace *Lobelia erinus* 'Mrs. Clibran')

Late spring

8 *Nicotiana alata* 'Lime Green' (replace *Nicotiana alata* 'Sensation Mixed')

1 *Amaranthus caudatus* 'Viridis' (replaces one of the two *Amaranthus caudatus*)

2 *Cosmos bipinnatus* 'Sensation' Mixed Colors (replace *Reseda odorata*)

6 *Gypsophila elegans* (replace *Nigella damascena* 'Miss Jekyll Blue')

8 *Petunia* 'Super Cascade Lilac' (replace *Petunia multiflora* 'Resisto Mixed')

NICOTIANA (short)

COSMOS (medium)

GYPSOPHILA (short)

GODETIA (short)

PETUNIA (dwarf)

AMARANTHUS (medium)

Early to mid spring Sow godetia seeds following instructions for mignonette and nigella on page 134, covering them with a maximum $\frac{1}{4}$ inch of fine soil.

Mid to late spring Thin out the godetia seedlings to 6 inches apart, following the instructions for mignonette and nigella on page 134.

Late spring Plant the nicotiana, amaranthus, cosmos, gypsophila and petunias following the instructions for pelargoniums etc on page 135.

Early and mid summer Go over the bed once a week with pruning shears, cutting off the dead flowers just below the heads, to encourage new blooms. Weed the bed every two weeks, and trim the grass around the edge of the bed with shears if it is set in a lawn.

Late summer and early autumn When the flowers are finished pull out the plants. Remove any weeds and fork the bed over to leave it tidy for winter.

1 *Nicotiana*: Early summer–early autumn **2** *Amaranthus caudatus* **3** *Cosmos*: Mid–late summer **4** *Gypsophila*: Early–late summer **5** *Amaranthus candatus* 'Viridis': Early summer–early autumn **6** *Godetia*: Early–late summer **7** *Pelargonium* **8** *Malcolmia* **9** *Petunias*: Early–late summer

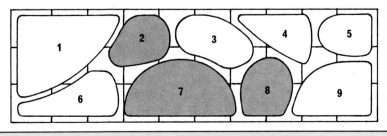

Foliage

This border is based largely on foliage effects. You will need the following additional plants. This variation does not require the Virginia stock.

Late spring

1 *Ricinus communis* (replaces *Nicotiana alata* 'Sensation Mixed')

1 *Humulus japonicus* 'Variegatus'

1 *Kochia trichophylla* (burning bush) (replaces one of the two *Amaranthus caudatus*)

8 *Pelargonium* 'Scarlet Diamond' (replace *Pelargonium* 'Rose Diamond')

6 *Tropaeolum majus* 'Climbing Mixed' (nasturtium) (replace *Nigella damascena* 'Miss Jekyll Blue')

5 *Coleus blumei* (replace *Petunia multiflora* 'Resisto Mixed')

12 *Lobelia erinus* 'Mrs. Clibran' (replace 15)

From the garden shed

Length of plastic-covered netting or wooden trellis measuring 6 foot × 4 foot

6 slender stakes 3 feet high

3 × 5 foot poles (if the border is backed by a hedge)

Packet of plant ties

Masonry nails or wire ties

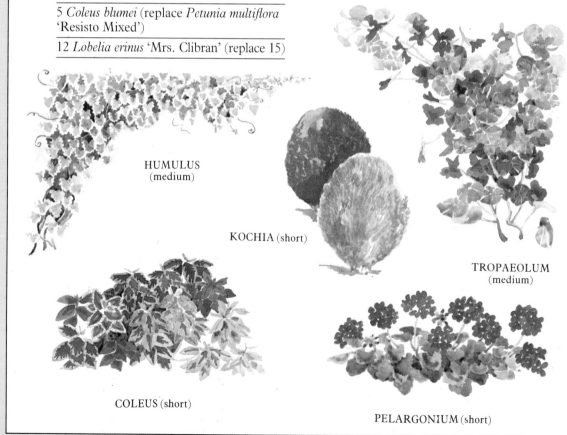

HUMULUS
(medium)

KOCHIA (short)

TROPAEOLUM
(medium)

COLEUS (short)

PELARGONIUM (short)

Method

Before marking the bed out, secure the netting or trellis in place at the back of the border where the climbing plants (nasturtium and humulus) are to grow. If the border backs on to a wall or fence it can be fixed to this using masonry nails or wire ties. If there is a hedge behind the border, hammer the three poles in position at the back of the border and secure the netting or trellis to those.

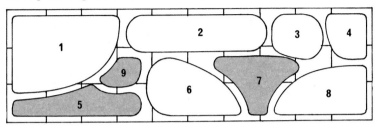

1 *Ricinus*   2 *Humulus*
3 *Nasturtium*: Early–late summer
4 *Kochia*   5 *Lobelia*
6 *Pelargonium*: Early–late
summer   7 *Mignonette*
8 *Coleus*   9 *Amaranthus*

Late spring To plant ricinus, burning bush, pelargonium, coleus and lobelia, follow the method described for the lobelia etc on page 134, but notice that the positions of some of the plants used in that plan have now changed. The mignonette has moved to the position previously occupied by the Virginia stock, and their original place is now occupied by nasturtium. Amaranthus has moved to the corner of the area occupied by the lobelia.

Plant the humulus and three of the nasturtiums close to their supports at the back of the border. The remaining three nasturtiums should be spaced out over the rest of their area.

RICINUS
(medium)

Early summer Push the slender stakes in between the humulus and nasturtiums, and as the plants start to grow encourage them to ramble up and over the stakes. If necessary hold them in place with plant ties.

Mid and late summer Add a new tie to the nasturtiums and humulus every two weeks to ensure the new growth is always held firmly in place. Do the same with the nasturtiums and humulus growing against the wall, tying them regularly up to the netting or trellis to "train" them in place.

Early autumn When the plants are starting to look past their best, pull them all out and – unless you plan to repeat the same border next year – take down the supports for the climbers.

With Perennials

This variation uses old-fashioned annuals offset by perennials chosen to provide a background of silvery or creamy foliage and white flowers to create a charming cottagey border. Substitute the following perennials and annuals for the plants shown in brackets.

Early to mid spring

1 *Gypsophila paniculata*, and
1 *Phlox paniculata* 'White Admiral'
　(replace the two *Amaranthus caudatus*)

5 *Hosta fortunei* 'Albopicta' (replace *Lobelia erinus* 'Mrs. Clibran')

3 *Stachys lanata* (replace *Malcolmia maritima*)

Mid to late spring

10 *Lathyrus odoratus* 'Jet Set Mixed' (sweet peas) (replace *Reseda odorata*)

From the garden shed

10 slender stakes 4 feet high

GYPSOPHILA
(medium)

HOSTA (short)

LATHYRUS (tall)

STACHYS (dwarf)

PHLOX (short)

Early to mid spring   Plant out the gypsophila, phlox, hosta and stachys using the method described for pelargoniums on page 135.

Mid to late spring   Plant out the sweet peas using the method described for nicotiana etc on page 134. Push the stakes in between the plants. There is no need to use ties as they will scramble up the stakes by putting out tendrils.

Early summer   Check that the sweet peas are growing up the sticks and are not entangling neighboring plants or running along the ground.

Mid summer   Deadhead the sweet peas, using pruning shears, as soon as the flowers are over or they will quickly stop producing new buds.

Early autumn   Pull up the sweet peas as they begin to die.

Late autumn   Cut back the flowers, stems and foliage of the gypsophila, phlox, hosta and stachys when they die back, using pruning shears. Weed the bed and leave it tidy for winter.

1 *Nicotiana*   **2** *Gypsophila*: Early–late summer   **3** *Sweet peas*: Early–late summer   **4** *Nigella*   **5** *Phlox*: Mid–late summer   **6** *Hosta*: Mid–late summer   **7** *Pelargonium*   **8** *Stachys*: Mid summer   **9** *Petunias*

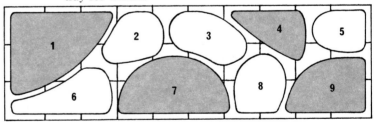

Water Gardens

Ponds are enormously adaptable, varying in character from the very formal to the totally informal, so there is one to suit every kind of garden. This chapter provides a selection of the different basic styles of water garden. The main plan is for a traditional semi-formal pond that contains something of interest for most of the year. Choose plants that are green and healthy-looking without any brown marks or rotting leaves, and where possible buy from a reputable water garden center or mail order water garden nursery.

Ingredients for a pond 8 foot × 6 foot with paving around the edges

Mid to late spring

1 *Nymphaea* 'James Brydon' (waterlily)
3 *Iris pseudacorus* (water iris)
3 *Typha minima* (dwarf cattail)
5 *Acorus calamus* (sweet flag)
5 *Scirpus albescens* (white bullrush)
3 *Hydrocleys nymphoides* (water poppy)
Elodea canadensis (optional)
Cabomba caroliana (optional)
6 *Myriophyllum aquatica* (parrot's feather)
1 *Nymphoides cristatum* (white snowflake)
Fish (optional)

From the garden shed

1 × 8 foot × 6 foot pre-formed plastic pond liner
$\frac{1}{2}$ cubic yard of building sand
Paving slabs and cement to surround the pool
Fertilizer tablets formulated for waterlilies

Tools required

Spade
Garden fork
Rake
Hose
Trowel
Piece of timber
Spirit level

Method

Choose a sunny location for the pond, well away from overhanging trees.

Buy a pond liner that is graduated in three steps so as to provide different depths of water when the pond is filled. The most useful graduations would provide water 24 inches, 12 inches and 6 inches deep.

Construct the pond by digging out a hole several inches bigger all round than the pre-formed pond liner you have bought. Use a spade to form the rough shape and size of the pond and finish off with a trowel to give a smooth, even finish. Make sure there are no stones sticking out of the soil.

Spread a 2 inch layer of sieved building sand evenly over the surface of the shape you have dug out. This is to provide a soft, cushioned layer to support the pond liner when it is full of water without the risk of sharp stones eventually penetrating it and making the pond leak.

Check to see how good a fit your liner is in the hole. To do this, first rake the sand lightly to leave the surface slightly indented by the points of the teeth. Now fit the liner into the hole and run a little water into it. Then bail it out, remove the liner and look at the sand to see which areas have been compressed by the weight of the water and which have not. You will be able to see easily where you need to add extra sand or remove some to achieve a perfect fit.

You will probably have to adjust the pond several times until you get a tight fit between the liner and the sand, but it is very well worth doing so. A good fit makes certain the liner is properly

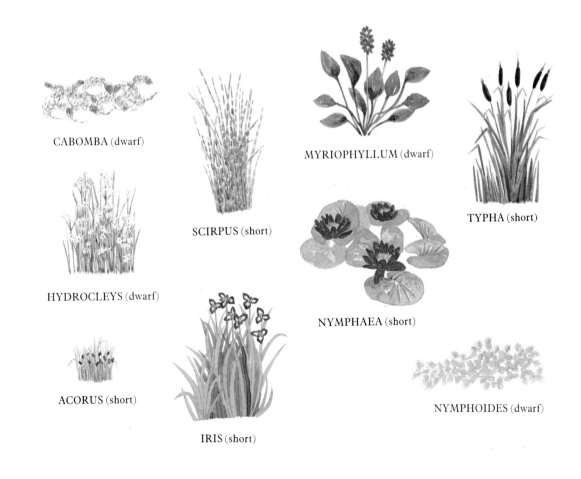

CABOMBA (dwarf)

MYRIOPHYLLUM (dwarf)

SCIRPUS (short)

TYPHA (short)

HYDROCLEYS (dwarf)

NYMPHAEA (short)

ACORUS (short)

NYMPHOIDES (dwarf)

IRIS (short)

supported all round, with no areas where the plastic is stressed by the weight it is carrying. This alone will considerably extend its life.

At the same time, check repeatedly to see that the liner is lying level in the ground. This is very important too, because if it is not the water will all run to one end! To ensure it is level, lay a piece of timber lengthwise across the liner and put a spirit level on it. Move the timber and spirit level through 90 degrees and see that the liner is level crosswise too. Make any adjustments that are necessary by adding or removing sand under the liner.

When the pool is properly fitted, lay the paving slabs around the edge and cement them in place. These can be formal paving slabs or pieces of irregularly-shaped crazy paving. You can either lay a single row of slabs around the pond or, if you prefer, continue it out to form a path or formal rectangular border around the pond. The purpose of making a border to the pond is partly to set the pond off nicely, and partly to conceal the edge of the liner which protrudes slightly above the level of the water. Lay the paving so that the edges overhang the sides of the pond slightly.

A week or two before you want to start planting, fill the pond with water so that it has a chance to warm up a little first.

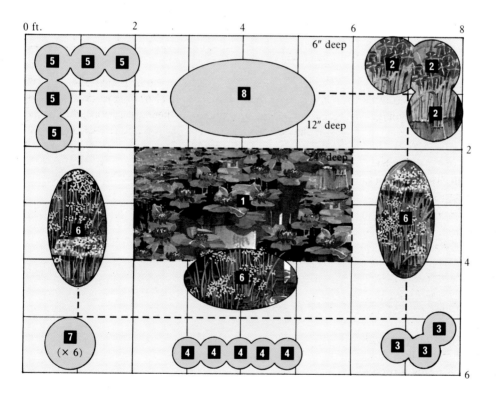

Opposite Pond. **Above** Plan for the pond. Colored areas indicate plants in flower in early summer. Average flowering periods are listed below: **1** *Nymphaea*: Summer **2** *Iris*: Late spring–early summer **3** *Typha*: Autumn **4** *Acorus*: Summer **5** *Scirpus*: Summer **6** *Hydrocleys*: Summer **7** *Myriophyllum* **8** *Nymphoides*: Summer

Mid to late spring

Planting   Water plants growing in containers need only to be lowered into position. Put them in as soon as you get home to avoid them drying out or "cooking" in plastic bags in the sun.

Square black plastic baskets are the usual containers for water plants. Check first to see that the containers are weighted and will stay where you put them. If they are not, place a handful or two of washed horticultural gravel on top of the soil in the container.

Plants that are bought in small pots need repotting into plastic tubs or pots large enough to accommodate them when full-grown. Choose black or brown containers if possible as they will not be visible when submerged.

Fill the container with heavy topsoil or garden soil that contains some clay. Knock the water plant out of its old pot by giving the base a sharp tap with the trowel. Make a hole the same size as the rootball in the soil in the new container and plant it into this, firming lightly down around the roots.

MAINTENANCE

Do not worry if the water in your pond turns green shortly after planting. It should clear itself naturally within a short time. If it does not, there are various chemicals you can add to clear it – ask at your nearest water garden nursery or aquarium supply shop.

(**Mid to late spring**)

Then secure the plant in place by running a length of wire over the rootball and twisting it around the sides of the container. This is to prevent the plant from floating out while its roots grow into the new soil.

Finally, place a handful or two of clean gravel over the top of the soil to prevent this too from floating out when the container is submerged. Before planting, water the container well, until the soil is really sloppy. It is now ready for planting in exactly the same way as those bought already prepared from a water garden nursery.

Plant standing at the edge of the pond rather than by stepping in, if possible, or there is some risk of cracking the liner. Start at the center and work your way out.

Plant the waterlily by lowering its container slowly into the center of the pond. It is essential that the leaves can float on the surface of the water. If the waterlily was previously growing in shallower water than that in your pond, you will find the leaves are pulled down under the water. If this happens, raise the lily container on a brick or upside down flower pot to start with, until its leaves can just float. From then on, each time the plant produces new leaves they will have slightly longer stems, and you can sink the container deeper into the water a little at a time until eventually it is resting on the bottom of the pond.

Simply place the containers of scirpus, iris, hydrocleys, myriophyllum, acorus, nymphoides and typha in position – these are upright plants whose leaves grow up out of the water, and provided they are planted at approximately the right depth (as shown in the plan) they will not need any special attention at planting time.

In subsequent years, divide plants that have become overgrown. Lift the containers out of the water and remove the plants. Divide the roots by tearing the clumps apart and replant the best piece in new soil in the same container. Handle the divisions as described earlier for planting new plants in containers.

Once a year, when the pond has become badly overgrown and in need of a spring-clean, remove all the plants, fish and water and scrub out the pond liner with clean water (don't use detergents as they may harm the plants or the fish). Refill with clean water and replant as before. Very occasionally you may need to take everything out to replace a cracked liner – the plastic slowly degrades and the pond starts to leak. When you find yourself refilling the pond very frequently (after about ten years) this is probably the case.

(Mid to late spring)

If you want to put fish in your water garden, add some submerged water plants such as *Elodea canadensis* or *Cabomba caroliana* for extra oxygenation. They remain under water all the time, giving a vague impression of massed green foliage in the bottom of the pond. They are sometimes supplied with weights attached, and can be placed into the pond near the center. You do not need to put them in pots.

Allow at least three weeks after planting the pond before introducing the fish. Buy only healthy fish from a reputable source; avoid any that are sluggish or have white spots on them. Bring them home in plastic bags full of water, tied at the neck, and float the bags in the pond for several hours before releasing them. This is to allow them to acclimate slowly to the change in water temperature. Remember to feed the fish regularly during the summer – the dealer should recommend the best food.

Throughout summer

Refill the pond whenever the water level drops by more than a few inches. Keep it regularly topped up.

Feed the waterlily once a month with fertilizer tablets especially formulated for waterlilies.

Early autumn

Feed the fish well.

Remove dead leaves from the surface with a net.

Pull the dead flowers and foliage from the waterlily. Remove any dead leaves from the other plants in the pond to keep it free of decaying vegetation.

> **In subsequent years**, thin out the oxygenating plants (myriophyllum, elodea and cabomba) in early to mid autumn to prevent an excessive build-up of vegetation in the pond.

Mid autumn

Cut down the seed heads of iris and typha close to water level.

Winter

Stop feeding the fish. Top the pond up with water.

If the water freezes over, make a hole in the ice by standing a bowl of hot water on top. Don't use a hammer.

Wildlife Pond

The traditional pond contained a mixture of plants designed to make it as ornamental as possible. However, for a wild garden or for a natural feature in a very informal part of a garden, a completely different style of pond is called for. A "wildlife pond" relies on an informal shape and plenty of native plants both in and out of the water to re-create the untamed look of a natural beauty spot, and provide a habitat for many water-loving creatures.

Mid spring

2 *Hydrocleys nymphoides* (water poppy) (instead of 3)

1 *Butomus umbellatus* (flowering rush)

1 *Meynanthes trifoliata* (bog bean)

5 *Lythrum salicaria* (purple loosestrife)

12 *Iris ensata*

3 *Valeriana officinalis* (valerian)

1 *Hydrocharis morsus-ranae* (frogbit)

1 *Caltha palustris* (marsh marigold)

10 *Myosotis scorpioides* (forget-me-not)

5 *Eleocharis monteridensis* (spike rush)

You will also need

An asymmetrical pre-formed pond liner with the sides graduated in two stages to provide different depths of water – 6 inches and 24 inches – when the pond is filled

50 × 2 gallon bucketfuls peat moss or well-rotted garden compost

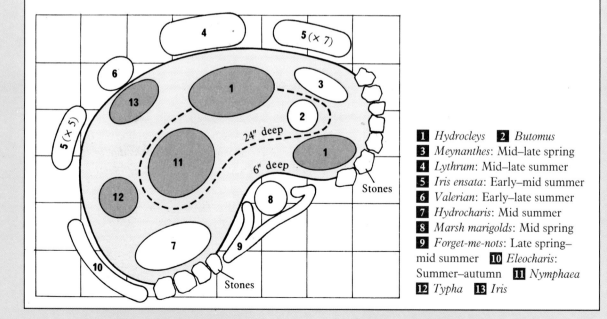

1 *Hydrocleys* **2** *Butomus*
3 *Meynanthes*: Mid–late spring
4 *Lythrum*: Mid–late summer
5 *Iris ensata*: Early–mid summer
6 *Valerian*: Early–late summer
7 *Hydrocharis*: Mid summer
8 *Marsh marigolds*: Mid spring
9 *Forget-me-nots*: Late spring–
mid summer **10** *Eleocharis*:
Summer–autumn **11** *Nymphaea*
12 *Typha* **13** *Iris*

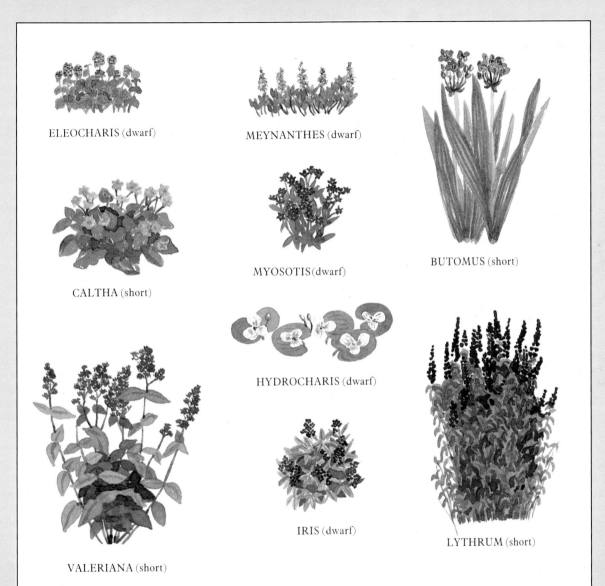

ELEOCHARIS (dwarf)

MEYNANTHES (dwarf)

BUTOMUS (short)

CALTHA (short)

MYOSOTIS (dwarf)

HYDROCHARIS (dwarf)

VALERIANA (short)

IRIS (dwarf)

LYTHRUM (short)

Method

Construct the pond as on pages 145 and 146 but this time without putting a complete border of paving around the edge. Instead, sink it slightly deeper into the ground so that the edge of the liner can be concealed under the foliage of surrounding plants, and use a few informally placed pieces of flat paving stone to complete the edge as shown.

After planting the pond itself (see left) prepare the surroundings. Dig in 2 bucketfuls per square yard of peat moss or well-rotted garden compost. Do not use manure or fertilizer in case it gets into the pond and turns the water green. Rake the ground roughly level.

Butomus, meynanthes, lythrum, iris, valerian, marsh marigolds, forget-me-nots and spike rush are all plants that love moist soil and will be planted around the edges of the pond. They are available from water garden, wildflower, and perennial plant nurseries.

Mid spring Hydrocharis is a floating plant and should just be dropped into the water in the required place.

Place the butomus, meynanthes, lythrum, iris, valerian, marsh marigolds, forget-me-nots and spike rush in their planting positions so the leaves of those closest to the pond just overlap the edge of the liner. When you are happy with the positioning, dig holes the same size as the pot, knock the plants out by tapping the base with a trowel and set them into the holes. Firm the soil lightly down around the roots and water the plants in very thoroughly.

If you cannot obtain plants, buy seed instead, available from specialist suppliers. This should be sprinkled thinly on to prepared and raked soil. Rake over the area lightly with the back of the rake and water well.

In subsequent years, remove surplus hydrocharis buds.

Some of the marginals (the plants surrounding the pond) may seed themselves and produce lots of seedlings. Leave some of these to grow and increase the natural look of the pond surroundings. Remove any that spread too far or too thickly. Remember, though, a wildlife pond such as this looks more authentic if allowed to become well populated.

Late spring When the seedlings come up after a few weeks, thin them out – you can, if you like, leave more than those shown on the plan to achieve a naturalized look more quickly. Keep the marginal plants around the edge of the pond very well watered.

Early autumn Cut the foliage and dead flower stems of the plants at the water's edge back almost to ground level when they start to die off naturally. Remove the debris from the area, and keep the pond free from decaying vegetation.

Replacement and additional plants are given at the start of each variation. For quantities of original plants, uncolored in the planting plan and not given in the variation ingredients, check with the list at the start of the main plan.

Boggy Banks

The first variation used moisture-loving native plants to naturalize the fringes of a wildlife pond. Here the same idea has been adapted to suit a more conventional garden pond, using moisture-loving herbaceous plants with the original "traditional pond" plants to create a pond with its own bog garden. To the plants in the original list, add the following:

Mid spring

4 *Hosta sieboldiana* 'Elegans'

2 *Sagittaria latifolia* (arrowhead)

1 *Rheum palmatum*

1 *Lobelia cardinalis*

6 *Myosotis scorpioides* (forget-me-not)

2 *Primula japonica*

2 *Astilbe* 'Fanal'

3 *Pontederia cordata* (pickerel rush)

1 *Typha laxmannii* (graceful cattail)

3 *Iris ensata*

You will also need

A rectangular piece of heavy black plastic pond lining material measuring 20 feet × 15 feet

Builder's sand

TYPHA (short)

ASTILBE (short)

PONTEDERIA (short)

MYOSOTIS (dwarf)

RHEUM (short)

IRIS (dwarf)

HOSTA (dwarf)

PRIMULA(short)

LOBELIA(short)

SAGITTARIA (short)

Method

The method of pond construction used here is very different to that for a conventional pond. There is no well-defined edge to this pond; instead, it merges gently into the surrounding bog garden which is kept permanently moist with water overflowing from the pond.

Start by clearing the area of weeds and digging the soil. Do not add any manure, compost or peat moss. Rake the soil roughly level and use the point of a stick to mark out the shape of the pond and the plant area surrounding it, as shown on the plan.

Then dig out the soil. Begin with the pond – the center should be 24 inches deep for the waterlily, and the edges 6 inches deep for the shallow-water plants. Make the edges of the pond at normal ground level, or only 1 inch below it. Check as you work to see that the edges of the pond are reasonably level, using the timber and spirit level method described on page 146.

Then continue the excavation outside the pond to form the shapes of the spaces allocated for the surrounding plants. These should be about 9 inches deep. Do not worry about excavating the entire area where the rheum is to go – just taper the dug-out area away into that corner.

Leave a reasonably flat surface when you finish the digging, and check there are no stones protruding from the soil. Then spread a layer of builder's sand 1–2 inches deep over the area which will be occupied by the pond. There is no need to do this for the surrounding garden area.

Next lay the plastic liner over the area so that it overlaps the pond by roughly equal amounts in all directions. It should also completely cover all of the planting areas.

Run a little water into the pool with the hose. As the pond begins to fill, you will see that the sheet is slowly pulled to the center by the weight of water as it takes up the shape of the pond. If the sheet is drawn too far to one side, exposing part of the planting area, pull it carefully back over. You may need to reposition the sheet slightly in this way several times before it is right. When it seems to be correct fill the pond completely.

Use part of the topsoil that was excavated, mixed with a few bucketfuls of peat moss, to fill in the pockets in the liner around the edge of the pond where plants are to go, so creating the bog garden.

Use a sharp knife to trim away the surplus lining sheet from around the edges of the area, and dig the edges into the ground to hide them.

Now take a sharp skewer and perforate the liner every 6–12 inches over the area of the bog garden. This is to provide some slight drainage, leaving the soil at just the right degree of bogginess.

When you have done this, run some more water into the pond. Keep filling until it overflows the edges, flooding into the bog garden areas.

Finally, place some paving stones around the edge of the pond at the positions shown on the plan. The garden is now ready for planting.

Mid spring Plant the pond first, following the method described on pages 147 and 148. Work standing on the stones at the side of the pond, so as to avoid either stepping in it (when you risk tearing the lining sheet), or treading in the bog garden around the edge.

Plant the edges of the pond afterwards. Stand the hosta, sagittaria, rheum, lobelia, forget-me-not, primula, astilbe, typha, pontederia and iris in position, and make a hole for each one big enough to take its rootball. Knock the plants out of their pots by giving the base a sharp tap with the trowel, or cut them away if they are the flexible black plastic type, and plant them into the holes. Firm gently around the roots, and water each plant individually to settle the soil round them.

Check every week to see that the bog garden is wet enough and replenish the pond with water whenever the level starts to drop to ensure the garden is kept watered too.

Do not use slug traps in the bog garden. Hostas are the plants most susceptible to slugs, though lobelia and astilbe are quite attractive to them too. They can, however, be protected by using slug traps in the rest of the garden, so preventing slugs from reaching the pond. It is also worth searching for slugs in the area and picking them up by hand. Birds coming to drink at the pool will do a good job of clearing slugs.

Late spring to early summer Cut down the flower stems of iris and primula as soon as the flowers are over.

Check every week that the bog garden is wet, and keep the water level in the pond topped up.

Throughout summer Continue checking the bog garden for wetness, and top up the water level when necessary.

Early autumn Cut down the old flower stems and foliage of forget-me-not, iris, pontederia, astilbe and hosta, and the foliage of primula when the plants start to die back.

Mid autumn Cut down the old leaves and flowers of rheum when they have started to die away naturally. In cold areas, cover the roots with a thick layer of shredded leaves or straw for the winter.

Cut down the old flower stems and foliage of lobelia when the flowers are finished and the plant starts to die back naturally.

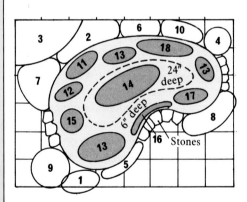

1 *Hostas*: Late summer **2** *Sagittaria*: Summer **3** *Rheum*: Early summer **4** *Lobelia*: Summer **5** *Forget-me-nots*: Late spring–mid summer **6** *Primulas*: Mid–late spring **7** *Astilbes*: Early–mid summer **8** *Pontederia*: Spring–early autumn **9** *Typha laxmannii*: Late summer–early autumn **10** *Iris ensata*: Early–mid summer **11** *Iris* **12** *Nymphoides* **13** *Hydrocleys* **14** *Nymphaea* **15** *Typha minima* **16** *Acorus* **17** *Myriophyllum* **18** *Scirpus*

Circular Pond

This variation is for a very formal water feature and would suit a small town garden or provide a focal point in a semi-formal garden. It makes use of the same range of plants in the main plan. You will not need myriophyllum and nymphoides.

You will also need

An ornamental stone cherub or other statuary on a plinth

Bricks and cement to complete edging

A pre-formed liner which provides a depth of 6 inches (which may, in a deeper pool, be made by raised shelves or platforms) and an area 24 inches deep

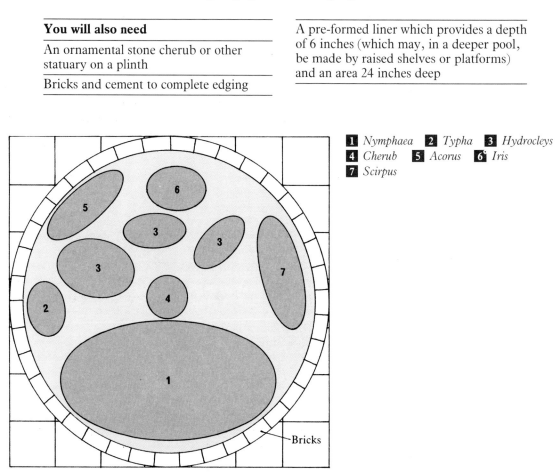

1 *Nymphaea*   **2** *Typha*   **3** *Hydrocleys*
4 *Cherub*   **5** *Acorus*   **6** *Iris*
7 *Scirpus*

Bricks

Method

Construct the pond following the instructions on pages 145 and 146 and finish it off by building a raised brick surround, one brick high, all around the pond to hide the liner and provide a formal edging. Maintenance and planting are as described in the main plan on pages 147 to 149.

Pond for Fish

The final variation is designed to provide a natural, healthy environment for fish that also looks attractive to us. It uses lots of oxygenating plants and species with large leaves to give fish shade and security from predators – plus a cozy nursery for their young. Overall, it gives a more informal feel to the rectangular pond in the main plan.

1 *Cabomba cardiniana* (replaces *Nymphaea* 'James Brydon')

1 *Myriophyllum aquatica*

1 *Vallisneria americana* (eelgrass)

3 *Crinum americanum* (bog lily) (replace *Typha minima*)

5 *Caltha palustris* (marsh marigold) (replace *Acorus calamus*)

1 *Cyperus alternifolius* (umbrella palm) (replaces *Scirpus albescens*)

3 *Pontederia cordata* (pickerel rush) (replace *Myriophyllum aquatica*)

3 *Hydrocleys nymphoides* (water poppy) (replace *Nymphoides cristatum*)

MYRIOPHYLLUM
(dwarf)

PONTEDERIA
(short)

CYPERUS (short)

VALLISNERIA (dwarf)

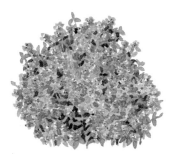

CRINUM (short)

CALTHA (dwarf)

CABOMBA (dwarf)

Method

Construct and plant the pond as described in the original plan on pages 145–148.

Do not introduce the fish for at least three weeks after planting the pond, to give the plants time to establish. In selecting the fish choose brightly colored species that frequently come to the surface – Koi carp or traditional goldfish – so that they are easily visible. If you wish to add snails to help keep the pond clean (their eggs will provide extra high-protein food for the fish), choose black Japanese snails or freshwater winkles, which will not feed on your plants.

Spring and summer Remove plant debris that falls in the pond, or dead leaves and flowers of water plants growing in it. Take care lawn clippings etc do not get into the pond; decomposing vegetation produces gases which are harmful to fish. Do not use weedkillers or fertilizers near the pond, and take care not to use them anywhere in the garden on windy days as even minute quantities blown into the water may also be harmful.

> **In subsequent years**, thin out excess growth of myriophyllum and vallisneria. Bog lily will need to be replanted each spring.

Autumn Take particular care to remove dead foliage and flowers from the pond and remove fallen leaves. Protect the pond by covering it with a net, if necessary.

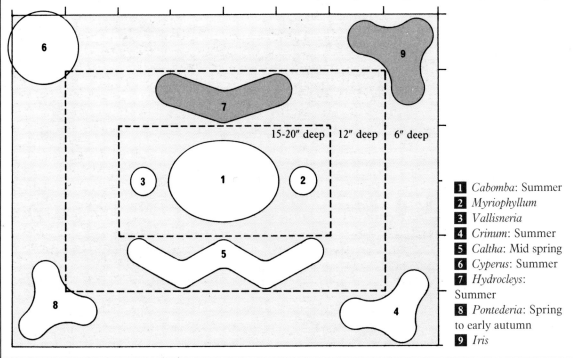

15-20" deep | 12" deep | 6" deep

1 *Cabomba*: Summer
2 *Myriophyllum*
3 *Vallisneria*
4 *Crinum*: Summer
5 *Caltha*: Mid spring
6 *Cyperus*: Summer
7 *Hydrocleys*: Summer
8 *Pontederia*: Spring to early autumn
9 *Iris*

Woodland Gardens

"Wild" gardens have recently become very popular and if you have an area of woodland clearing you are already halfway there. By selecting plants that enjoy the conditions and arranging them informally you can achieve a garden that looks as if it grew naturally. The main plan is for a naturalistic garden in a woodland clearing with a light tree canopy and slightly dry soil. The variations give planting schemes for other soil types. Very little pruning or attention is necessary in these gardens.

Ingredients for a clearing 20 foot × 10 foot

Mid spring

12 *Potentilla fruticosa* 'Abbotswood'

3 *Alchemilla mollis*

4 *Arundinaria disticha* (bamboo)

1 *Sambucus canadensis* 'Plumosa Aurea'

3 *Berberis* 'Atropurpurea'

1 *Mahonia aquifolium*

8 *Hedera helix*

Early autumn

24 *Anemone blanda*

From the garden shed

18 × 2 gallon bucketfuls of peat moss, garden compost or well-rotted manure

4–5 pounds 5–10–5 or other all-purpose fertilizer

44 × 2 gallon bucketfuls of bark chips, garden compost or leaf mold for mulching (optional)

Few lengths of fallen tree or logs

Tools required

Spade

Garden fork

Mattock (optional)

Rake

Hand trowel

Watering can or hose

Garden line or 4 stakes and string

SAMBUCUS (tall)

HEDERA (dwarf)

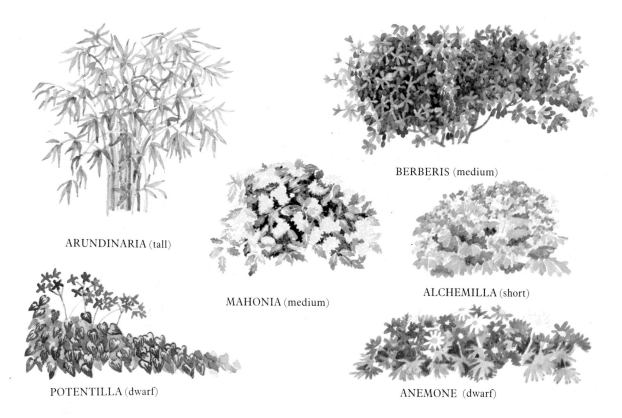

ARUNDINARIA (tall)

BERBERIS (medium)

MAHONIA (medium)

ALCHEMILLA (short)

POTENTILLA (dwarf)

ANEMONE (dwarf)

Method

The method of preparing the soil is rather different for a woodland garden than for a normal garden bed.

Start by clearing any undergrowth such as brambles, nettles, tree seedlings etc from the area, but leave all the existing trees and saplings surrounding it. Do not remove any of the natural leaf litter.

Mark the boundary of the "bed" out with a garden line or four stakes and a piece of string. Then divide the area into squares measuring a yard each way, using the point of a stick to leave a slight impression in the soil. This gives a guide for marking the positions where the plants are to go. Push a short stake in place for each plant. Then remove the line.

Do not cut an edge around the garden, as this is to be an informal garden, in which the plants are "naturalized" into the surrounding woodland. As the plants grow they will soften the edges of the basic rectangular shape, and blend gently into surrounding trees.

After marking the planting positions, place a few fallen logs to outline the pathway through the clearing, as shown on the plan overleaf.

Prepare the soil where alchemilla, potentilla and hedera are to go by spreading 2 bucketfuls per square yard of peat moss, compost or manure and forking it into the top few inches of soil. It will be difficult to go deeper than this because of the tree roots you will almost certainly find there. Follow this up by sprinkling fertilizer evenly over the area at 2–3 pounds per 100 square feet, and raking the ground roughly level.

It is not necessary to prepare the entire area of ground where the mahonia, berberis, arundinaria, and sambucus are to go as is normally done for a traditional bed. Here it will be sufficient to prepare the soil at each planting position, and leave the ground between as it is.

Mid spring

Before planting Stand the mahonia,
berberis, bamboo and sambucus next to
the stakes that mark their positions and
have ready one bucketful of peat moss,
well-rotted manure or garden compost
and about 1 cup of fertilizer for each
plant. Mix the two together so that the
fertilizer is evenly distributed
throughout.

Planting Dig holes in the positions
marked by the stakes, about twice the
size of the roots of the plant that is to go
into each one. Pile the soil you dig out
into a heap alongside each hole. Fork
over the soil at the bottom of the hole to
loosen it and tip in half the bucketful of
compost and fertilizer mixture. Stir this

MAINTENANCE

Mulch the entire area by spreading a thin layer of bark
chip, peat moss, or well-rotted garden compost or leaf
mold over the soil surface. Alternatively, if there is
sufficient natural leaf mold and litter available in the
woodland surrounding your clearing this could be used
instead. The path between the plants should also be
covered with the mulching material. This is partly to
prevent weeds from coming up and partly to complete the
natural look of the surface.

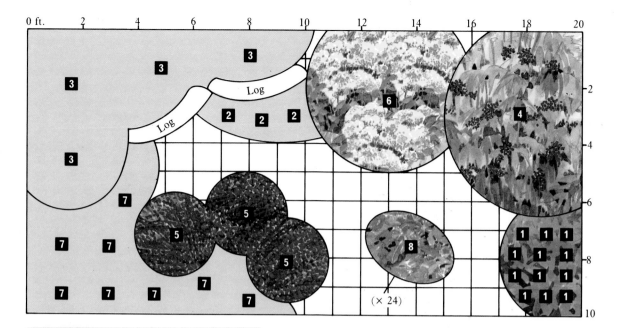

0 ft. 2 4 6 8 10 12 14 16 18 20

Log

Log

(× 24)

(Mid spring)
with a fork to mix it into the loose soil at the bottom of the hole. Add the remaining mixture in the bucket to the heap of soil at the side of the hole and mix them together. This will be used for filling in around the roots when you plant.

To knock plants out of rigid containers, just tap the base with the back of the trowel first. Containers made of flexible plastic should be carefully cut away without damaging the ball of roots inside.

Place the rootballs of the mahonia, berberis, bamboo and sambucus in the center of the holes you have made. Place a short stake over the hole to see if the top of the rootball is level with the surrounding soil. If it is not, then either remove soil from the bottom of the hole or add some from the pile alongside it until the top is level.

Then fill in round the roots with the rest of the soil/compost mixture. Firm gently down around the plant with your foot to consolidate the soil slightly.

Plant the alchemilla, potentilla and hedera by digging a hole the same

Opposite Woodland garden.   **Above** Plan for the garden. Colored areas indicate plants in flower in spring. Average flowering periods are listed below: **1** *Potentilla*: Late spring **2** *Alchemilla*: Early summer–late summer **3** *Arundinaria* **4** *Sambucus*: Late spring–mid summer **5** *Berberis*: Foliage spring–summer **6** *Mahonia*: Early spring–mid spring **7** *Hedera* **8** *Anemones*: Early–mid spring

In subsequent years, dig up and divide clumps of bamboo when the old plants start to become too big – this will be quite a major undertaking as the roots become very densely matted together. A mattock is the implement traditionally used for dividing bamboos, but if you do not happen to have one try using two strong garden forks back to back instead, aided by an old bow saw or a large knife to help cut through the root mass. Replant those sections of roots with plenty of new young growth from around the outside of the original clump.

Alchemilla may also be divided when the clumps start to grow large and elderly.

Prune mahonia, berberis and sambucus only to remove dead, frost-damaged or misshapen branches. Cut these back to a natural junction with another branch.

Cut back hedera if it starts to become too invasive but, ideally, it should be encouraged to spread out of the garden and into the neighboring woodland.

(Mid spring)
size as the pot and fitting the rootball into it. Make sure the top of the rootball is level with the surrounding soil. Fill in around the roots with soil and firm it down with the handle of the trowel.

Water the plants to settle the soil around the roots. Give the mahonia, berberis, bamboo and sambucus about 1 gallon of water each, and the alchemilla, potentilla and hedera about 2 pints each.

Late spring through late summer

Water the new plants whenever the soil around them feels dry. Check every week and water as often as necessary. This will help the plants to become well established and start them growing quickly. You will probably find that plants in a woodland need more water than those in a border to start with; the trees will take a great deal of water from the soil, which will consequently dry out faster than normal.

Weed whenever necessary, though the combination of natural shade plus the mulch will be sufficient to prevent most normal annual weed seeds from germinating.

Strong-growing perennial weeds such as nettles and brambles may be a problem, however. Dab the leaves with a weedkilling stick (available from nurseries and garden centers) as soon as they appear. If they have been allowed to become large, cut them off at ground level and dab the new growth when it appears. This avoids disturbing the plants they are growing among and is also much easier than trying to dig them out of ground filled with tree roots. Do make sure not to let any weedkiller get on to the leaves of the cultivated plants. If this does happen, wash the leaves thoroughly with water.

Early autumn

Planting Plant the anemone corms by digging a hole 3 inches deep and dropping a corm into the bottom of each – do not worry about getting them the right way up as it is not possible to tell which it is. Fill the holes in with soil.

Cut down the dead flower stems and old foliage of alchemilla, but leave the new foliage growing at the center of the plant.

VARIATION ONE
Acid Soil

Acid soil should not be regarded as a problem but as the means of growing a huge range of exotic and colorful acid-loving plants such as camellias and rhododendrons.

Mid spring

3 *Pernettya mucronata* (replace *Berberis* 'Atropurpurea')

1 *Fothergilla major* (replaces *Mahonia aquifolium*)

1 *Pieris japonica* 'Variegata' (replaces *Potentilla fruticosa*)

4 *Gaultheria procumbens* (replace *Alchemilla mollis* and *Anemone blanda*)

28 *Pachysandra terminalis* 'Variegata' (replace *Hedera helix*)

Mid autumn

1 *Camellia* 'Donation', in warm climates or 1 *Rhododendron kiusianum* (replaces *Sambucus canadensis* 'Plumosa Aurea')

4 *Rhododendron yakushimanum* (replace *Arundinaria disticha*)

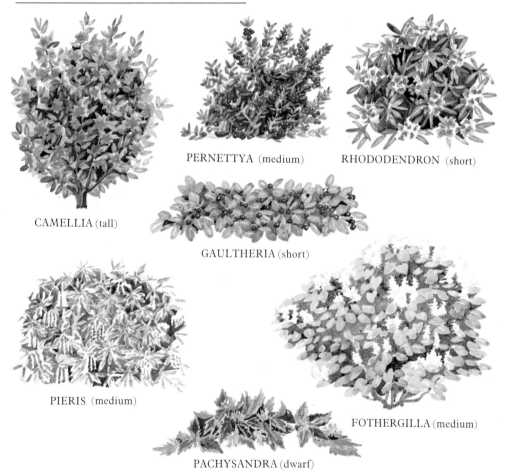

PERNETTYA (medium)

RHODODENDRON (short)

CAMELLIA (tall)

GAULTHERIA (short)

PIERIS (medium)

FOTHERGILLA (medium)

PACHYSANDRA (dwarf)

Method

Before planting it is a good idea to check your soil to see that it really is sufficiently acid. Either send a sample off for analysis (your local USDA County Extension office can give you materials and instructions for preparing a soil sample for testing), or buy a soil test kit and do it yourself.

When gathering soil for analysis, either at home or at a laboratory, it is very important to make sure the sample is truly representative of the area to be planted. Soil analysis often produces misleading results when the soil is all taken from one place. To collect a good sample, take a trowel and a large plastic bag and dig a series of holes to the full depth of the trowel all over the area to be planted, about 2 yards apart. Scoop a small sample of soil from the bottom of each hole and mix all the samples together in the plastic bag. Remove a small quantity to test.

To grow the acid-loving plants in this plan, you will need a soil with a pH of 4.5–6.5. At pH 6.5, soil is described as only slightly acid. In this case it may be advisable to use acid peat moss to increase the acidity of the soil when planting instead of manure or compost.

Mid spring   Plant the pernettya, fothergilla, pieris, gaultheria and pachysandra following the instructions on page 162.

> Replacement and additional plants are given at the start of each variation. For quantities of original plants, uncolored in the planting plan and not given in the variation ingredients, check with the list at the start of the main plan.

Mid autumn   Plant the rhododendrons and the camellia if you live where camellias are hardy outdoors. Follow the planting instructions on page 162.

> **In subsequent years**, mulch round rhododendron, pieris and camellia by spreading moist peat moss around each trunk, extending as far as the canopy of leaves.
>
> Pruning is not generally necessary other than to remove any dead or damaged branches.

Late spring   Weed and water following the instructions on page 164.

> **In subsequent years**, deadhead rhododendron and camellia by nipping off the dead flowerheads between thumb and forefinger rather than with pruning shears. This is because the new shoots that will carry next year's flowers grow out from just below the old flower heads and they are easily cut off by mistake with pruning shears.

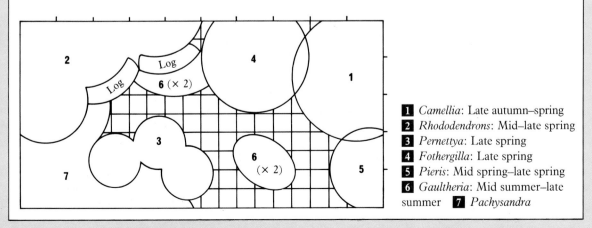

1 *Camellia*: Late autumn–spring
2 *Rhododendrons*: Mid–late spring
3 *Pernettya*: Late spring
4 *Fothergilla*: Late spring
5 *Pieris*: Mid spring–late spring
6 *Gaultheria*: Mid summer–late summer   7 *Pachysandra*

Alkaline Soil

This variation is for a different kind of "problem" soil – this time alkaline, which gardeners usually describe as "sweet", though it does not actually smell sweet. Do not attempt to alter the pH of your soil if it is naturally acid.

Mid spring

1 *Daphne mezereum* (replaces *Potentilla fruticosa* 'Abbotswood')

4 *Euonymus fortunei* 'Emerald 'n' Gold' (replace *Alchemilla mollis* and *Anemone blanda*)

3 *Cotoneaster dammeri* 'Skogholm' (replace *Berberis* 'Atropurpurea')

COTONEASTER (tall)

EUONYMUS (short)

DAPHNE (short)

Mid spring Prepare the ground and plant the daphne, euonymus and cotoneaster following the instructions for mahonia etc on page 162.

In subsequent years, prune cotoneaster if the plants get too big by reducing the length of overlong branches. Do the same if the plants grow out of shape.

Daphne is very slow growing and the only pruning that will be needed is if any branches die back. Cut back to a natural joint with a well-shaped, healthy branch.

1 *Euonymus* **2** *Cotoneaster*: Early autumn–late autumn **3** *Daphne*: Late winter–early spring **4** *Sambucus* **5** *Hedera* **6** *Arundinaria* **7** *Mahonia*

Damp Soil

This "problem" soil is the best kind for a woodland garden, and the variation takes advantage of this to create a damp, shady garden that will provide a range of color all year round.

Mid spring

5 *Primula japonica* (replace *Alchemilla mollis*)

1 *Gunnera manicata* (replaces 3 *Arundinaria disticha*)

1 *Acer palmatum* 'Atropurpureum',
3 *Hosta fortunei* 'Albopicta', and
5 *Primula polyanthus*
(replace *Berberis* 'Atropurpurea')

1 *Viburnum plicatum* (replaces *Mahonia aquifolium*)

3 *Peltiphyllum peltatum* (replace 1 *Arundinaria disticha*)

Early autumn

24 *Galanthus nivalis* (snowdrops) and
12 *Erythronium dens-canis*
  (replace *Anemone blanda*)

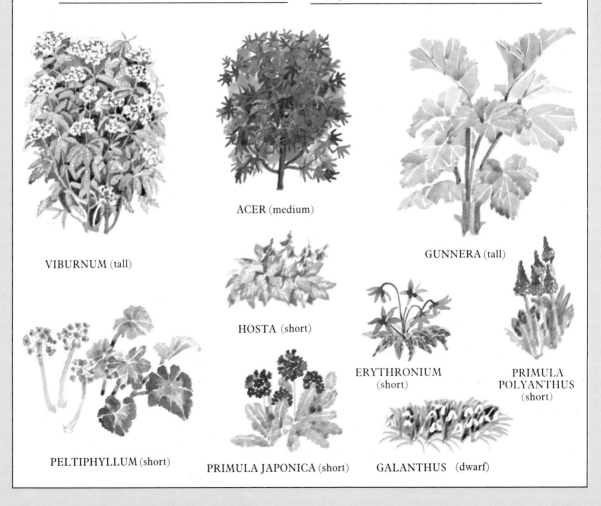

ACER (medium)

VIBURNUM (tall)

GUNNERA (tall)

HOSTA (short)

ERYTHRONIUM
(short)

PRIMULA
POLYANTHUS
(short)

PELTIPHYLLUM (short)

PRIMULA JAPONICA (short)

GALANTHUS   (dwarf)

Mid spring   Plant out the primulas, gunnera, hosta and peltiphyllum following the instructions for alchemilla etc on page 163. Plant acer and viburnum following instructions for mahonia etc on page 162.

Early autumn   Plant the snowdrop and erythronium bulbs in clumps of two, three or four over the area allocated to them for a nice natural effect. Dig out individual holes, which should be approximately 2 times as deep as the bulb itself. Put a little peat moss or compost at the bottom of the hole and plant by pressing each bulb gently into it. Then fill the hole in with soil or a mixture of soil and peat moss.

In subsequent years, allow the dead flower heads to remain on *Primula japonica* so it can set seed. These will fall and should grow into new plants without any intervention. Dig up the seedlings and replant in the correct position to replace the parents.

Early to mid summer   Cut down the flower stems of peltiphyllum and primula when the flowers are over.

Towards the end of September, cut down the old foliage of hosta when it starts to die back naturally.

Mid autumn   Cut down the old leaves and flowers of gunnera when they have started to die away naturally. In cold areas, cover the roots with a thick layer of peat moss or evergreen branches for the winter.

Cut down the old leaves of peltiphyllum when they start to die back naturally, after making the most of their brilliant autumn coloring.

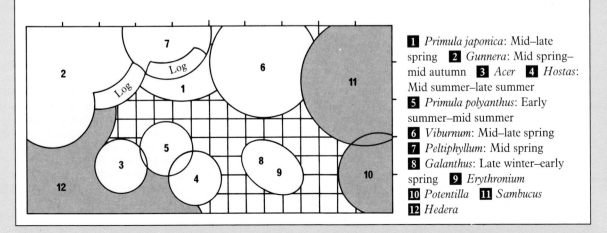

1 *Primula japonica*: Mid–late spring 2 *Gunnera*: Mid spring–mid autumn 3 *Acer* 4 *Hostas*: Mid summer–late summer 5 *Primula polyanthus*: Early summer–mid summer 6 *Viburnum*: Mid–late spring 7 *Peltiphyllum*: Mid spring 8 *Galanthus*: Late winter–early spring 9 *Erythronium* 10 *Potentilla* 11 *Sambucus* 12 *Hedera*

Wildflower Garden

Conventional shrubs and groundcovers are omitted from this variation and replaced with wild flowers, bought as plants or seeds, to create an authentic woodland clearing.

Early spring

3 *Dipsacus fullonum* (teasel) (replace *Potentilla fruticosa* 'Abbotswood')

5 *Primula elatior* (oxslip) (replace *Alchemilla mollis*)

12 *Digitalis purpurea* (foxglove) (replace *Arundinaria disticha*)

3 *Silene schafta* (moss campion) and 12 *Stellaria holostea* (greater stitchwort) (replace *Berberis* 'Atropurpurea')

6 *Viola odorata* (violet) and 6 *Fragaria vesca* (wild strawberry) (replace *Anemone blanda*)

12 *Epilobium angustifolium* (rose bay willow herb) (replace *Mahonia aquifolium* and *Sambucus canadensis* 'Plumosa Aurea')

24 *Scilla hispanica* (Spanish bluebells) (replace *Hedera helix*)

DIPSACUS (medium)

PRIMULA (short)

SILENE (short)

DIGITALIS (medium)

EPILOBIUM (medium)

STELLARIA (short)

VIOLA (dwarf)

FRAGARIA (dwarf)

SCILLA (dwarf)

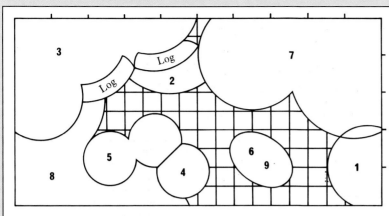

1 *Dipsacus*: Mid–late summer
2 *Primulas*: Mid–late spring
3 *Foxgloves*: Mid–late summer
4 *Silene*: Early–late summer
5 *Stellaria*: Mid spring–early summer　6 *Violets*: Mid–late spring　7 *Epilobium*: Mid–late summer　8 *Scilla*: Mid–late spring　9 *Fragaria*

Early spring If you buy plants, mark out the ground and planting positions as suggested in the original plan. Dig a hole twice the size of each plant's root-ball and mix a spadeful of peat moss or compost into the bottom. Use a mixture of soil and compost or peat moss to fill in around the roots, as on page 163.

If you buy seeds, clear the ground of weeds and debris and roughly fork compost into the top 3–4 inches; use the same total quantity as stated in our original plan. Rake the ground level, and scatter the seed.

Rake over the same ground again, but very lightly this time so as to just cover the seeds with soil. Then water, and leave well alone.

Mid autumn To plant the bluebells, dig a hole three times the depth of each "bulb" and drop a handful of compost into the bottom. Then press the bluebell firmly into it before filling the hole with a mixture of soil and compost.

In subsequent years, replace dipsacus with new plants, as they are biennial and die after flowering. You should only need to replace them once, as in following years the original plants will have seeded and self-sown seedlings will appear. This will also happen with the other wildflowers you have introduced, so that they gradually naturalize over the whole area; any that come up where you do not want them can however be pulled out.

Mid to late spring If the seedlings look crowded when they emerge, thin them by pulling out the weakest-looking ones. Otherwise nothing further is necessary.

Cut down the dead flower stems of digitalis and epilobium. Leave the teasels of dipsacus as winter ornamentation.

Index

Printed in italy by Milanostampa Farigliano (CN)

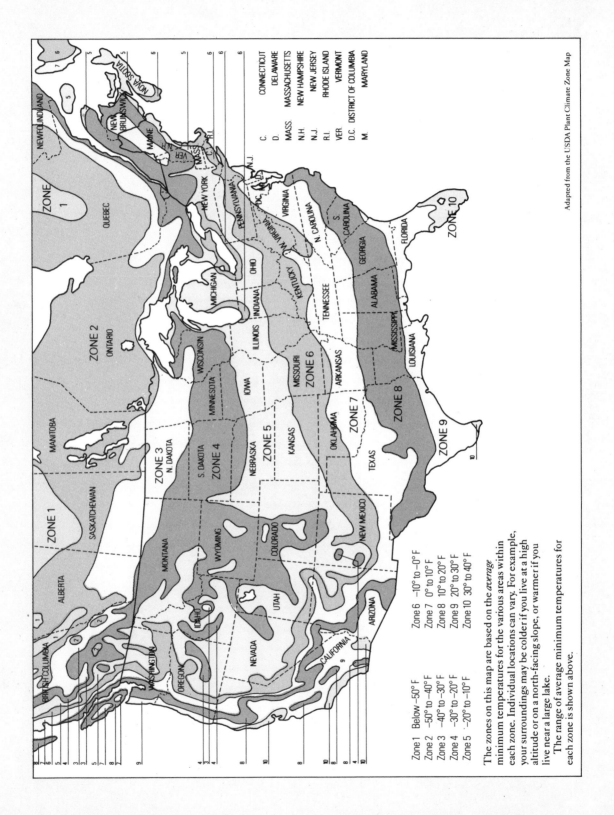

Zone 1   Below −50° F
Zone 2   −50° to −40° F
Zone 3   −40° to −30° F
Zone 4   −30° to −20° F
Zone 5   −20° to −10° F

Zone 6   −10° to −0° F
Zone 7   0° to 10° F
Zone 8   10° to 20° F
Zone 9   20° to 30° F
Zone 10 30° to 40° F

The zones on this map are based on the *average* minimum temperatures for the various areas within each zone. Individual locations can vary. For example, your surroundings may be colder if you live at a high altitude or on a north-facing slope, or warmer if you live near a large lake.

The range of average minimum temperatures for each zone is shown above.

C.   CONNECTICUT
D.   DELAWARE
MASS. MASSACHUSETTS
N.H.   NEW HAMPSHIRE
N.J.   NEW JERSEY
R.I.   RHODE ISLAND
VER.   VERMONT
D.C.   DISTRICT OF COLUMBIA
M.   MARYLAND

Adapted from the USDA Plant Climate Zone Map